Mark Regan

Tim Rodber

Tom Smith

Tim Stimpson

Alan Tait

Gregor Townsend

Tony Underwood

Rob Wainwright

Paul Wallace

Doddie Weir

Barry Williams

Keith Wood

David Young

Mike Catt

Nigel Redman

Tony Diprose

Kyran Bracken

Tony Stanger

 # HEROES ALL

THE OFFICIAL BOOK OF THE LIONS IN SOUTH AFRICA 1997

IAN McGEECHAN

with Mick Cleary

Introduction by
WILLIE JOHN McBRIDE

Photographs by
Colin Elsey and Stuart Macfarlane
(COLORSPORT)

Additional photographs from
REUTERS

Hodder & Stoughton

First published in 1997 by
Hodder and Stoughton
A division of Hodder Headline plc

10 9 8 7 6 5 4 3 2 1

ISBN 0 340 70740 2

A CIP Catalogue record is available
for this title from the British Library

Produced by Lennard Books
A division of Lennard Associates Limited
Mackerye End, Harpenden, Herts, AL5 5DR

Production Editor: Chris Hawkes
Text and cover design: Design 2 Print
Reproduction: The Colour Edge

Printed and bound in Slovenia

Hodder and Stoughton
A division of Hodder Headline plc
338 Euston Road
London NW1 3BH

ACKNOWLEDGEMENTS

I would like to thank Reuters and MBN Promotions for their major sponsorship
of this book and also all the other companies which have generously supported the
book with their advertising. Without such tremendous assistance it
would not have been possible to have such a glossy publication.

I would also like to pay a special tribute to Mick Cleary, rugby correspondent
of the *Daily Telegraph*, for his immense help in the preparation and editing of this book.
Very grateful thanks to Colorsport for their excellent photographic selection of
the highlights of the tour – well done Stuart Macfarlane and Colin Elsey.
Thanks too to our other pictorial contributor, Reuters.

I would like to thank Ian Robertson for arranging the interviews with
Fran Cotton, Martin Johnson and Kitch Christie in the Reflections chapter
and also for his help in compiling the Reuters Dream Lions team.

I am indebted to the willing band of typists, spearheaded by Lisa Tytler and Clare
Robertson who transcribed over half a million words and who prepared the final manuscript.

I would like to pay special tribute to Adrian Stephenson for all his encouragement
and help in this exciting project and finally I would like to thank the entire
British Lions squad for playing so magnificently to ensure the Lions won a
Test series in South Africa for only the second time this century.

CONTENTS

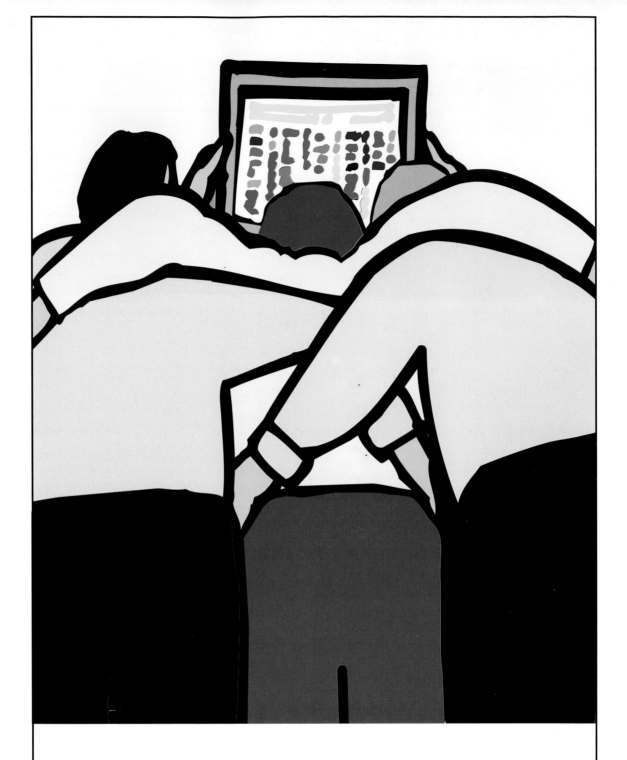

When it comes to passing information, we're in front of the pack.

REUTERS

Foreword
by Julie Holland – Managing Director, Reuters UK and Ireland

Lions tours are always remarkable for one reason or another, if only for their rarity. This one was the first in the new era of professional rugby and came at the end of the longest domestic season ever. The tour was also comparatively short yet the itinerary notably intense with some 13 matches in seven weeks. Commentators and pundits were encouraging but expected the squad to struggle with some of the provincial matches and not win the Test series.

I will leave it to you to decide on the tour high spot, be it John Bentley's storming try during the Gauteng Lions match which Fran Cotton described as a defining moment, Matt Dawson's dummy which fooled four Springboks or my own, Jeremy Guscott's drop goal which secured the Test series. All truly magic moments.

As well as supplying the global financial and corporate markets with information and data, Reuters is the leading international sports news agency. Our dedicated team in London monitors some 50 different sports worldwide and is supported by numerous specialists and local freelance stringers in our 163 international bureaux. Daily, Reuters publishes on average 100 sports stories, including frequent updates on major sporting events.

Our 120 photographers, located around the world, ensure that the 500 or so pictures published daily by Reuters are the most comprehensive and topical. Many of the pictures in the national press of the Lions Test matches were taken by Reuters photographers – two are below.

Reuters is delighted to support this publication as well as sponsoring the Reuters Dream Lions team, a concept dreamt up by Mike Newlin of MBN Promotions.

This book is a fitting testimony and record of a truly unforgettable tour, with its unique atmosphere and the final remarkable result.

virgin atlantic

Introduction
by Willie John McBride

I was lucky enough to go on five British Lions tours between 1962 and 1974 and I am delighted to say that after we had failed to win a single Test match during the 1962 and 1968 tours to South Africa or the 1966 tour to New Zealand, life took a decided turn for the better in 1971 and 1974.

I thought at the time that winning the Test series against the All Blacks would be an unbeatable experience but I was wrong. The greatest highlight of my whole rugby career was leading the British Lions on the twenty-two-match unbeaten tour of South Africa where we won the first three Tests and drew the last.

It was an unforgettable three-month safari with a phenomenal group of thirty players united by a burning desire to prove that the four Home Unions could produce great players and a great team spirit. We had total commitment to the cause and we never wavered once in our determination to win the Test series. My abiding memory is not of fifteen players winning the Test but a squad of thirty players all combining together and supporting each other to bring out the best in everyone.

This summer in South Africa, as I travelled round the last four weeks of the Lions tour, it almost seemed as if time were standing still and history was repeating itself.

The 1997 Lions produced not only a great Test team but also an outstanding unbeaten midweek side who pushed the Test players all the way through the seven weeks in South Africa. The Lions management admitted that the selection for the first Test was the most difficult job they had ever had to do with twenty-five players right there in contention and very little separating them.

They played exciting rugby and fulfilled all their huge potential to clinch the Test series 2–0 with wins in Cape Town and Durban. To show how difficult it is to win a Test series in South Africa just look at the history books. In the first ninety-seven years of the twentieth century only two major touring teams had previously won a Test series in South Africa – the 1974 Lions and the All Blacks in 1996.

That puts into perspective the magnitude of the remarkable achievement of these 1997 British Lions. It has been an outstanding story of glorious success for northern hemisphere rugby and underlines what I have preached for over thirty years – to play for the British Lions is, and always will be, the ultimate pinnacle for any rugby player from England, Scotland, Ireland and Wales. Long may Lions tours continue. They are very special and very important for the future of the game.

This pride of Lions has restored pride to British and Irish rugby. The players responded to the challenge superbly. So did the coach, Ian McGeechan. He masterminded the Lions Test series win in Australia in 1989, and he was in charge for the narrow 2–1 defeat in New Zealand in 1993. He has been the most successful coach in the northern hemisphere for the past decade and this is his story of how the Lions humbled the Springboks. It is a story well worth telling.

Willie John McBride.

1. PREPARING FOR THE SPRINGBOKS

The offer did not require much thought. Yes, I had done it before. And, yes, too, there were commitments at Northampton to take on board. But the Lions are still something very, very special. In this frenetic, busy new world of professionalism there are not too many fixed points. People say to me that the Lions do not really fit into the scheme of things any more. To my mind, that is complete and utter rubbish. The British and Irish Lions are a sacred institution, one which is unique in the whole world of rugby and even across the whole of sport. That is why I did not think twice when approached in the summer of 1996. If the Lions wanted me, then it was an honour and a privilege to accept.

The Lions have always had a particular magic for me. Little has changed since I first toured with them as a player in 1974. The tours may be much shorter these days – we were away for four months in '74 – but the magic is still the same. I think Clive Rowlands summed it up best. He was the manager when I first coached the Lions in 1989. I remember him addressing the squad then, shortly after we had assembled for Australia. In his passionate Welsh tones he held up the Lions badge on the shirt. He said that the badge would either get bigger or smaller by whatever we did on the field or off it. He was absolutely right. The badge would be enhanced or diminished by our every action. That squad grew right through the tour and my mind often went back to Clive's words. They capture the essence of the Lions.

People forget that the Lions vintage of each particular year does not exist until the players

Ian McGeechan in South Africa with the 1974 Lions.

actually meet up. The Lions of '97 had no character, no identity, no meaning until we met at the Oatlands Hotel in Weybridge a few days prior to departure. The players make it what it is. They lend their own characters and identities and it all fuses into one. That is why the Lions are so unique.

Even though I had spent many hours talking with the other selectors about the various players and had watched several of them at close quarters in the English league, I had no real idea how the squad would react to those around them and to the challenge ahead. A player reacts differently when there is someone else alongside him. Even the great players have to adapt. They have to make the others tick so that they themselves can perform. So you have this marvellous process whereby everyone is on their toes, nervous and excited because it is an unknown adventure.

Most of the players are experienced internationals. Yet they will be going suddenly into a different, more testing environment. These days international sides are more and more like club teams. They meet so often, have so much time together, that there is a chance to develop gradually. There is a fair chunk of fixed personnel in any international side which lends stability. The evolution is slow-moving, the process a rolling one. The Lions could not be more different. With them it is an instant process. Either it comes together or it does not – either it meshes or it does not. It is such a narrow window of opportunity. There are no second chances. The Lions have a lifespan of eight weeks. Then they are gone.

This is why the hair on the back of my neck prickled when I thought of the team running out at Port Elizabeth for the first match. It was still the best part of twelve months away, but that is the pull of the badge, the magic of the whole challenge. It is an intense experience. You simply cannot come to a Lions tour in a half-hearted frame of mind. You have to immerse yourself in the whole thing. You have to become part of the country you are travelling through. You have to accept the atmosphere you find there because you have helped to create it. It may be hostile, feverish, alien – but you are partly responsible for it and you should accept it. Everyone will want a piece of your time. That can be a hassle but, again, you need to embrace

it. They are excited and interested and keen because you are there. When I went down to South Africa to watch the series against New Zealand in 1996, they were already talking about the Lions. Rugby means that much down there.

For our players it is a step up in status and awareness. In South Africa, as in New Zealand, rugby is king. That alone is fantastic. It also means that the Lions are something else altogether. The South Africans appreciate their unique value. They too can get tired of the same old rugby diet. The Lions freshen the palate. It is perhaps a shame that there is now so little scope to go up-country. The schedule is too tight and unforgiving. In the old days we would head off to some backwater, meet the locals and recharge the batteries. But, much as we are aware of the need to mix with the locals, there is simply not the time available to do it in the old manner. Our main objective is to win the series and the itinerary allows for little or no distractions.

The key thing for both player and coach is to come with an open mind. You have to react to what is around you. That was one of the critical criteria I outlined for selection. You wanted players who would be strong and decisive – guys who are not afraid to take things into their own hands and get on with it. That was the hallmark of the 1989 squad. It was full of strong individuals. I sensed from an early point that the 1997 party were made of similar stuff.

Going to South Africa is a huge challenge for any side. It is quite staggering that it took the All Blacks so long to win a Test series there. They only finally got the better of the Boks in 1996. I do not know why that should be. Partly it must be that South Africa is such a different culture from all the other major rugby-playing countries. It is a vast, stark place with variable climates, conditions, pitches, backdrops and attitudes. From liberal Cape Town to conservative high veldt – nowhere else demands so much of you. The one common factor is that the South Africans are a hard race and their rugby players are fearsome physical specimens. A Springbok is a big, big man.

These were some of the thoughts we threw around in our meetings throughout the year. It was a great comfort for me to know that there was such a high-quality, conscientious selection panel. I just did not have the time available to get round all the matches I might ideally have wanted to see. My duties at Northampton took priority during the season, although I did, of course, come into contact with many of the candidates for selection in the course of the Courage Division One games. I knew in my own mind the type of player we were looking for in every position. I had gone down to South Africa the summer before to see at first hand just what lay in wait for us. The Home Unions committee financed the trip, a sign of their professional intent. It had never been done before. The trip was invaluable.

The All Blacks were in the country and they could not have been more helpful. I had several meetings with their coach, John Hart, who I knew well, and also their captain, Sean Fitzpatrick. They were so open and honest. Sean pointed out the great benefit of having a bigger squad than the normal thirty. The All Blacks had travelled with thirty-five, which allowed the core position players such as Fitzpatrick at hooker to have a match off. In the past they had always found themselves on the bench as cover. It was on their recommendation that I proposed to the Home Unions that we too should take a thirty-five-man squad. John Hart and I talked long and hard about what it took to beat the Springboks on their home patch. The All Blacks had thoroughly vetted every hotel and every training facility. We did too, Fran Cotton going down for a twelve-day reconnaissance to make sure that everything was just as we wanted it. We also had the biggest back-up squad the Lions have ever taken.

This may all sound trivial in cold print, but believe me I saw what a difference it made to the All Blacks. They were thoroughly professional in their approach. It was no coincidence that they played that way on the pitch too. John Hart also stressed the need for us to be totally self-contained. On his advice we sent all our own training kit ahead of us. Scrummage machine, rucking and mauling machines, body-tackle padding, tackle bags – the whole lot went off ahead of us in a container ship. This gave us complete control over all our training. It gave us a sense of strength and independence too.

There are certain fundamentals about taking on South Africa. John and I discussed at length just what strategies might best help us to beat them. The New Zealanders obviously got their homework right. Their series victory was emphatic. First of all, you have got to have the power to confront them. You also have to be mentally strong to take them on; you need players who are tough and resilient just to cope with being on a long tour as well as strong-willed enough not to be fazed by anything that happens once the tour has begun. Above all else I wanted players who were decision-makers, ones who were not afraid to play it as they saw it at that moment in time. The Springboks showed in winning the World Cup in 1995 that they were the best defensive side in the world. We had to break them down and the only way to do that was to have talented players who were thinkers, who could react off each other and to different circumstances.

We could not have players who would show any weakness because the South Africans would be on to them in a flash. The forwards, then, had to be aggressive. This did not mean that I wanted them to pile in at every opportunity. Far from it. There would be no '99 calls' on this tour (the famous sign to start a mass brawl). The game has moved on enormously from those days of mayhem in 1974. You need control and self-discipline, not a wild, unpredictable approach which would create more problems than it would solve. The game is so much more closely policed these days that players just cannot get away with being thugs. As Fran Cotton said in the wake of the disgraceful incident which put Doddie Weir out of the tour, the simple difference between 1997 and 1974 was that they did not have press conferences in the old days. So much went on unnoticed and unremarked upon. I thought the attitude of our players at Mpumalanga when Doddie was so viciously taken out of the game – and, sadly, the tour – was first-class. They maintained their composure and focus. The best reply to that sort of brutality is to point to the scoreboard. I reckon that ten tries and 64 points was all the retaliation they needed.

For the tour selection I drew up a list of requirements for each position and then tried to match the players available against those criteria. You are rarely going to get the perfect specimen so the whole exercise is a matter of trimming, adjusting and redefining. We went into much more detail on every thing and every one – far more so than we had in 1989 and 1993. I did have the players together for a bit longer beforehand on those two tours but that apart the 1997 tour was far more meticulously planned. We were given more scope and the necessary finance to be able to do it, particularly through the funding of my trip to South Africa in 1996. That visit shaped my whole outlook. I worked out my playing philosophy from watching the Boks at close quarters and from those invaluable talks with the New Zealanders. The criteria for selection derived directly from this playing philosophy.

I wanted to play a game that the South Africans did not expect us to play. I wanted us to be fluid and dynamic, to play on the edge as often as possible. That did not mean we would be loose but it did mean that we would not play in a straitjacket. The southern hemisphere teams tend to think of northern hemisphere teams as predictable, cautious and one-dimensional. That perspective was going to change. I had seen from the way the All Blacks beat the Boks that you needed to destructure the game so that the predetermined defensive patterns were broken down. That meant that we couldn't really play to a plan ourselves. There were no plans A and B, just a format. The players had to play the game as they saw it before them – in short, to make decisions on the move. They had to get in and out of contact quickly in order to keep the ball on the move.

If all this were to work then the players had to be ambitious, they had to want to take themselves out of their own comfort zone, to challenge themselves and each other. The thought of players going back home at the end of the tour without having really gone for it, of having failed to achieve because they had been afraid to try, appalled me. Jim Telfer and I were as one on this – we would never tear a player off a strip for doing something in a match as long as he believed it to be right and went for it 100 per cent.

All this was determined nine months before we set out. Shortly after that I had fifteen to twenty of the names pencilled in. A few faces were to change during the year as form came and went or newcomers such as Eric Miller appeared on the scene. But I had my vision of

A great season with Leicester and Ireland brought Eric Miller into consideration.

what I wanted to do – it was just a question of finding the right people to do it for me.

The Rugby League contingent became an increasingly important factor during the course of the season. They were well-versed in playing the sort of game I wanted – power allied to pace. In the forwards we needed ball-handlers. That said, you could not ignore the essentials either because if your scrummage is being badly messed about then you are usually going nowhere.

We spent a lot of time talking to the various club coaches about their players. We knew a fair amount from watching them play, but for a successful tour you need more than just a guy who can play a bit of rugby. You need players to combine with others, in a social as much as a sporting sense. The '97 Lions had no team spirit whatsoever when they met up at Weybridge. They had to find it within a few days or we had no chance. That is why a player's character was also so important.

Take John Bentley for example. People were surprised when he made the squad. I do not really know why. He had so many of the qualities we were looking for. He was a hard runner on the pitch and a terrific bloke off it. Fran knew him from old, but still we spoke to those around him who confirmed that John was a great asset in a large group. He was popular but also very professional. Like all the ex-League players he was a real talker on the field, always communicating with those around. John and the others – Alan Tait, Scott Gibbs, Allan Bateman, Scott Quinnell and David Young – also had a magnificent attitude to training. They were very, very professional in everything they did, which is what I wanted to rub off on all the others. It did.

Jeremy Guscott's skills were known from old, but did he still have the desire?

the highlights of the tour. There was fierce fighting for position between them all which is just what we wanted. That is why I could never quite understand the fuss when Phil de Glanville was left out of the large sixty-two-man initial squad. You only had to consider those who did make it to appreciate how much quality we had in the centres.

Will Greenwood made the squad, Jim Mallinder of Sale did not. Jim, though, was very close indeed. He is such a strong runner, the sort of bloke who can come from the back and really mean it. But Jim's prospects were compromised by our need for goal-kickers. It was as cruel as that. The fly-half and full-back

Will Greenwood continued to impress throughout the course of the season.

There were others players we marked down early on. There were the obvious choices, I guess, like Jeremy Guscott. This was my third Lions tour with Jerry. He is one of my all-time favourite players. I knew he had the talent – all I needed to know was whether or not he had the inclination. It was no good having all that ability but not wanting to come. Jerry was in good order even though England had not picked him. I must say I could not understand why but in many ways it was to my advantage in that he would be hungrier than ever.

Will Greenwood was another who made an early impression. We had him marked down as far back as September. Will interests the opposition defence and makes space for those around him. He always looked comfortable on the ball which was just the attitude we wanted. The pressure for places in the centre was one of

conundrum took up a lot of our time. In the end we went for a balance between the creative need and the reliability of the place-kickers.

There was real jostling for places in the back row as well. I was determined to go with specialist open-side flankers. We could not play in the style I wanted without one. Richard Hill of Saracens was a name I had written down very early on – long before England had him in their team. He came through so well in the course of the season. He was big, powerful and

Martin Johnson was the logical choice as captain.

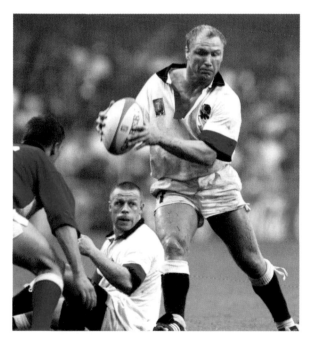

Used in the right way, Neil Back could flourish in the Lions' style of play.

intelligent. Neil Back was a late contender in some ways. Colin Charvis of Wales had made the running during the Five Nations, but then picked up a lot of injuries. I also knew Neil's capabilities of old. I admit that I had been swayed by the sizeist argument before, passing over Neil in 1993. The debate as to whether he

is big enough or not will rage on. For our purposes, however, Neil was the ideal choice. If you play him in a certain way, then there are few better. He is in and out of the contact so quickly, flipping the ball away before any of the opposition can get their hands on it. We had to produce situations where we could get the best out of Neil's abilities.

Finally, the captain. It was not a difficult decision. Martin Johnson fitted so many of the criteria we were looking for. He had the respect of all those around him and was one of the very few guaranteed his Test place. I also fancied the idea of Martin knocking on the door of the opposition to toss up. Every other captain would invariably be looking up to him. He was the Lions representative, strong, tall and steadfast. Above all else Martin had total credibility with the players. He is not one for fine speeches, although he surprised a few in that department, too. He leads by example, pulls others along with him. He was just the man.

There had been so much work put in before we even congregated. I was in touch with Fran almost every week. We had regular selection meetings, and planning sessions too which focused on playing strategies, training ideas and player development. Finally, the domestic season staggered to the tape. It had been a long haul and I have to admit I was concerned about how tired some of the players might be. You have to manage situations like that, however, and not let the constraints get to you. So, if they were worn out, then we would give them some time off. Martin Johnson was a case in point. I had already spoken to him and to Fran before we left about his missing the opening two games. Conversely there were some in the squad who had not played very much rugby at all in the run-up. Paul Grayson and Neil Jenkins were on their way back from injury, while someone like Keith Wood only had a handful of games under his belt.

It was obvious that we had to adapt and treat people accordingly. I think I was in a much better frame of mind myself to tackle these problems than I had been on previous Lions tours. I just did not feel the need to prove myself all the time. This meant that I could be more dispassionate and objective about these sorts of situations. A coach often wants to spend as much time as possible on the field or with the players. I realised here that I had to be strong enough not to do something, to back off if necessary. The players' welfare was the priority. If a session needed to be cancelled then it would be. We did so on the very first day we met up at Weybridge. We had achieved what I wanted to achieve so I let the boys go. The same thing happened a few days later. We were doing the right thing at the right time, not just because it was on the pre-ordained schedule.

Weybridge was an important staging post. Those first few days are crucial. People can be hesitant and edgy, unsure of how to react to each other. Some of these boys were knocking ten bells out of each other for their countries only a couple of months before. Weybridge had to be carefully planned. Above all else, it had to be different. Most of the players were stale after the long season. Even so we needed them to bond with each other as quickly as possible. I wanted that to happen but not through rugby activities. Fran had been put in touch with a couple of companies who specialise in the corporate market, devising means of making workforces more co-operative and productive. A company called Impact came up with a few ideas, we laid down the parameters, and the programme was born.

I had used a few of the strategies before in my time with the Scottish Life Assurance Company. However, I insisted that the sessions we had were to be practical and not based in a board-room. We split the players into teams throughout the work. The teams kept changing as we blended nationalities, positions and types. Tom Smith, for example, ended up with Jason Leonard – same position but completely different characters, Jason outgoing, Tom reserved. Eric Miller, the youngest in the squad at twenty-one, found himself alongside Ieuan Evans and Jeremy Guscott, the two most experienced Lions.

We had one set of teams for the Monday and Tuesday of that week, then changed again. There were lots of games and exercises, designed to build a sense of team spirit by getting people to work together. On the Monday evening we had a couple of ice-breakers. The squad, including all the back-up staff, was divided into teams of nine. They had a simple task – to all put their hands on a cane and then put it on the ground together. It sounds ridiculously easy but it is not. Everyone has to communicate with each other, some directing, others making decisions. Another exercise involved getting all the team through the holes of a spider's web, a big net which has different openings at different heights. Again you had to have someone taking a lead and others supporting and endorsing. Tuesday saw us trying to get a bucket of water on to a platform in no man's land. The teams had to work out a plan and then implement it. Through that day we also did work on how to get under ropes into someone else's territory. There was also a session where all the teams had to work together, so that everyone was now supportive rather then competitive.

By Wednesday I knew that we were on course. The squad was coming along wonderfully. Already there was a sense of this being a party of strong characters. That day was spent climbing trees with rope ladders, the highest being about sixty feet off the ground. Although it was all great fun, the players had to be responsible when the tasks involved risk. We did an exercise where the group had to build a tower of beer crates to see how high they could get. When Tom Smith toppled off ours (he was roped on) he was almost thirty feet in the air. There were canoe races out on the river which caused no end of amusement with the big fellas trying to straddle the canoes across a weir.

The whole emphasis was on finding out about each other, trying to create relationships in a relaxed environment. We were all aware though of the serious test which lay ahead. The squad

would be under more pressure than most of them had ever been exposed to. There was the media pressure to contend with too. On Thursday we had an open day with the media which was preceded by a talk from two journalists, David Norrie of the *News of the World* and John Taylor from the *Mail on Sunday*. The players had to understand what constraints and pressures the media had to work under, to try and see the job from their point of view.

The time to leave was drawing very close and you could sense the players beginning to focus on what awaited them in South Africa. We had a long session together where we laid down certain fundamentals. The management were also keen to stress to the players that it was their tour not ours. They would have to take the lead on many things. Fran, I and all the others were there to support them. I simply gave them the framework in which to operate. They were to add the meat, to decide the detail. We told them that there would be no meetings held just for the sake of it.

On the Friday before we left the squad drew up their own criteria – what became known as the 'Lions Laws'. They thrashed out a set of guiding principles for everyone, from the need to give people their own space, to appreciating different temperaments. They discussed the difficulties about being away from home for so long, about how players would need support if they were injured or dropped. There were thoughts too on dress codes, punctuality and a chat about alcohol. The guys also deliberated on how they would feel if they did not make the Test team. Everyone wants to be in the first XV, but they cannot all be in it. They had to consider how they would react to that. If they could deal with that then they could deal with anything.

By the end of that day they had come up with headings and bullet points for all these situations. They were typed onto a card and laminated in plastic so that all the squad could carry them around with them all the time, just pulling out the card as and when to remind them of what they had decided.

We all knew it would be difficult. There have only ever been three victorious Lions tours.

Every Lions team has left these shores as underdogs. It was nothing new. I was very confident though, if only because I felt relaxed. This was a good squad. Of that I was certain. The week had gone tremendously well. We only had a brief glimpse of glory. As we left London on Saturday evening, bound on a Virgin flight for Johannesburg, I knew that the 1997 Lions were going to give it one hell of a shot.

The 1997 'Lions Laws'.

1997 LIONS LAWS

DISCILPLINE

1. Small financial fines by the players court at players discretion.

2. Disciplinary committee empowered to be judge and jury on serious disciplinary matters. Formed from 4 people, FEC, IMcG, MJ, RW. Any decisions must be unanimous.

SELECTION AND POLARISATION

1. Non selected players should congratulate the player selected in his position.

2. Selected players to publicly recognise the role of non players.

3. Any selection queries are taken to the coach, not discussed with other players.

4. Before Tests on a strictly confidential basis, non selected players should be forewarned by the Management. For other games selection is announced at meetings only.

5. Focus must be maintained by all 35 players and coaches before every game especially the final two mid week games.

6. Make a concerted effort to get to know all members of the party, eg training, seating at dinner, etc.

7. Make the team room the focus of the party - not the bedrooms.

8. Once a week to go off site from the hotel to go out together.

9. Have one daily meal together as a squad, eg lunch.

10. Entertainment for people through non rugby related events.

INTERNAL/EXTERNAL COMMUNICATION

1. Bi weekly team meetings, Management to leave for last 10 minutes.

2. One to one objective feedback, training.

3. Opportunities for players to voice concerns through to Management via the selected senior players, LD, SG, MJ, AT, PW.

4. Cut off times for calls to Rooms 10.00 pm - 10.00 am. BB to vet any nuisance calls being put to the rooms.

6. Press conference. BB and MJ to nominate two/three players for conferences, but the players will have the final choice.

7. What happens on tour stays on tour.

TEAM SPIRIT

1. Back bone of the side, keeps us together whatever.

2. How will we know if we are getting it right? Mood in camp, the atmosphere, positive, smiling, enthusiasm.

3. Team spirit will motivate each other, drive standards and stop complacency.

4. The five senior players, LD, SG, MJ, AT, PW, appointed as team leaders who will have access at all times to the Management.

5. We should continue our non rugby team building in South Africa.

CODE OF CONDUCT

1. No one to go out on pre match nights.

2. Alcohol. Individual responsibilty, nothing that is detrimental to you or team performance.

3. Punctuality. Player input into itinerary.
No excuses for lateness unless it has been communicated beforehand.
Room mates take responsibilty.
Court to decide fines, etc.

4. Dress code
Training as instructed by coaching staff
Functions as requested
Travel is casual
Hotel is casual, but we have a duty to our sponsors
In free time, players responsibility, still have duty to sponsors.

Distractions
High risk activities check with medical officers. Each player is to prepare for games in his own way. Players who are not playing are not to distract playing members.
At training grounds, BB to control the press.

GET A

LITTLE

EXTRA

HELP

FROM

THE . . .

2. PLAYED FOUR, WON FOUR

The fun and games were over. The activities in Weybridge had been hard going in their own way, but the objective was to give everyone a break from the rigours of a long domestic season. The players needed to be refreshed and revitalised in a different environment. The Impact boys had done well. The squad had gelled wonderfully and there was a buzz about the group. The tone though was about to change.

The week in Durban was all about rugby. We would still have some laughs along the way but there was no doubt in anyone's mind that we had to find the necessary intensity and focus to beat the Springboks as quickly as possible. There is no ducking reality on a Lions tour. Time is short and opportunities are golden. The entire lifespan of a Lions group is two months. You live or die by what happens in that short space of time.

There was no need to spell this out to the players. They knew it better than anyone. They knew that they had to knit together as quickly as possible, to work out patterns of play, instinctive awareness of each other's inclinations, foibles, fallibility, moods and every last aspect that goes into grooving a good team as opposed to a collection of good individuals. They were prepared for work.

This was just as well. Durban was hot and the players were made to sweat. We had chosen a base about ten miles from the city centre at a resort called Umhlanga Rocks. It was a beautiful setting, the Beverly Hills Hotel jutting out towards the Indian Ocean where the surf crashed on to the rocks all day long. This was no lotus land though. We all trained together in the morning at King's Park before splitting into groups in the afternoon for work in the gym or the swimming pool. I do not think people quite realise how many component parts have to synchronise perfectly to make a good rugby side.

Take the forwards. You might have the best eight individual players in the world at your disposal, but there is no guarantee that they would go well against a decent provincial or even club side. The scrum and line out are all about co-ordination and timing; loose play too. If the players are just working to their own agendas then the pack will never perform with any real conviction or purpose. Jim Telfer took a couple of early scrummage sessions in Durban and only rated the performance as three out of ten. I was not too worried. There is a direct return on time invested when it comes to scrummaging. There was time yet to bruise some flesh on the scrum machine and on the training field later in the tour.

I wanted the players to switch on to a whole new attitude and awareness of where and how we wanted to play the game. Our aim was to beat the Springboks and each provincial game was to be a step towards that goal. Of course victory was important. By far the best preparation for the Test series was to arrive at it unbeaten. But we were attempting a change in rugby culture for our players and that was unlikely to happen overnight or necessarily very smoothly. We were going to play ball-in-hand and the biggest commitment to that cause would be demanded of the forwards, the front five in particular. I thought they responded magnificently.

The first game always has a special edge to it. It is a shame for the players in the second match because no one from outside views that occasion in quite the same light, yet for the players concerned, many of them making their Lions début, it is of course a unique event. So, to Port Elizabeth, a little later than was perhaps ideal. We had been always scheduled to arrive on Friday evening so as to maximise our training in one fixed spot in Durban. In retrospect, I felt it was a bit late. Perhaps it was just me getting anxious; the players did not seem at all fazed by it, not even when half the baggage went missing. It is so important when touring not to let the little things get to you. It might be a cramped bedroom, a pitifully weak shower, lost laundry – any one of a hundred things which might touch a raw nerve simply because you are a long way from home. The key thing is to just absorb it as part of the whole experience. These things will happen and you have to recognise how you are reacting to them. This squad was superb. They never complained about a thing.

The players were itching to get going against Eastern Province. We had a team meeting soon after we arrived at our seafront hotel. I led the session and just tried to draw together all the strands – what we had to do to make sure that all the theory came into being. We were all aware that we had to lay down early markers and give notice of what we were about. We were looking to play in and out of contact as quickly as possible. We needed quality ball from the set-piece and from the next phase of contact. These were the trigger points the players had to react to.

Selection for the match was done with a view to giving the entire squad a game, with the exception of Martin Johnson, by the end of the second game. We wanted to go for tried combinations in certain areas, for example Keith Wood and Jason Leonard in the front row, both Harlequins men. I was not too concerned about having to split up the different nationalities for it was already apparent that there were no cliques in this Lions party. I wanted to get Rob Howley and Gregor Townsend together as soon as possible. It would have been

Rob Howley was given an early opportunity to build a good relationship with Gregor Townsend.

crazy to wait too long to see what sort of partnership might evolve. It was a mouth-watering prospect. I had intended to reunite the 1993 Lions centre pairing of Jeremy Guscott and Scott Gibbs, but Scott had to pull out with a bruised knee. So in came Will Greenwood, the only uncapped player in the squad. It made for great copy, the journalists told us, pairing the two players that England had overlooked that season. Nick Beal and Ieaun Evans on the wings was a mix of the young and the old while Neil Jenkins at the back would, I was sure, give us great value with his goal-kicking.

Will Greenwood was paired with Jeremy Guscott for the opening match.

The selection committee was four strong – myself, Fran Cotton, Jim Telfer and Martin Johnson. Johnno was there to give his opinion rather than to vote formally, which it never came down to anyway. We had more or less made up our minds prior to departure that Martin would sit out the first couple of games. He was raring to go within himself, but recognised that the real goal was the Tests and that his body needed some recuperation after such an arduous season.

Port Elizabeth stirs all sorts of good memories. It was where we clinched the series in 1974 and had a famous wild night afterwards. It was peculiar to go back to the Boet Erasmus

stadium for the first time since. It has not changed much. The big bank of terracing is still there and the gangway down from the changing rooms to the field is just as I remembered it. The ground was only a ten-minute walk from the hotel, so Jim and I took a stroll up there in the morning just to check out the changing-rooms and medical facilities and the like.

By the time we got back to the hotel you could sense that there was an edge there. We did a few line out drills on the lawn in front of the hotel before heading for the final team meeting at 1.30, an hour and three-quarters before kick-off. It was here that Fran handed out the Lions shirts to the twenty-one players. It was a very special, emotional moment. There was absolute silence in the room as it dawned on everyone that all the speculation, all the months of build-up and hype was coming to a close. Soon it would be for real and there could be no more talking.

Fran and I told the players how we felt about being a British Lion in South Africa. How being a winning Lion would be a feeling that they would never, ever forget. At that moment in time the 1997 Lions had no credibility at all in South Africa. No one knew what they were made of. British rugby would either go up in the eyes of the locals or it would be laughed at. It was in our hands. We had to show the South Africans, and the world at large, that we could play rugby as well. The Super 12-type game was not, in my opinion and that of the squad, the preserve of the southern hemisphere. The message had to be from this match onwards that they would ignore us at their peril.

Eastern Province would be no pushover, however. They had a reputation for being hard and uncompromising – Tim Rodber had been sent off against them in a brutal match with England three years previously – and they also had some quality guests turning out for them, principally the two Springboks Hennie le Roux and Kobus Wiese, both of whom were anxious to impress after recent injury. They did not get much of a chance to impress, certainly not in the early stages.

We made a magnificent start. The first twenty minutes were almost perfect. Everything clicked into place as if we had been playing together for many years. Jeremy Guscott's try after just nine minutes was a beauty. It had everything in it – a back-row move, inter-passing, recycling at the breakdown, quick ball, long cut-out pass and Jerry drifting off his man and in under the posts. There were nine pairs of hands in evidence just up to the first breakdown. Even the heat did not seem to affect us. We ought to have scored again shortly afterwards but we did not and became loose and edgy. In later games, particularly against Mpumalanga, we did not let teams off the hook.

We put away our chances with real precision and shut the door on the opposition. Here we did not and Eastern Province sneaked back into contention with a couple of penalty goals before half-time. Neil Jenkins had notched an early one for us so it stood at 10–6 at the interval.

A lack of concentration had handed back the initiative to Eastern Province. The type of game we were trying to play requires enormous self-discipline. It may look as if everything is played off the cuff, but it is not. The sequences have been rehearsed time and again and the players have to be mentally very sharp to be in the right place at the right time.

There was a ten-minute interval, the first time we had come across it under the new laws. I went on to the pitch and told the players to keep it moving. There were a lot of points on offer here. I was quite happy with the way we were playing, so much so that even when their winger, Keyser, scored within a few minutes of the restart I was not too concerned. We had spoken time and again about how difficult it is

Half-time against Eastern Province and some words of encouragement from the coach.

to win games in South Africa. No side will allow you just to turn up and win. You have to fight for it. Our boys fought for it in that second half.

A few of the guys were getting physically distressed as the game wore on yet they still held their shape. We played superbly in those closing stages, putting players into space and not giving away possession in the turnover. Rob Howley, Gregor Townsend, Jerry Guscott and Will Greenwood cut some beautiful angles and it all fell into place. Doddie Weir scored from close range after getting under Wiese. Doddie had a terrific game against him, never letting him settle in the line out. In fact we won more ball on their throw than on our own.

We were already realising that the entire shape of the game had changed. The scrum had become a much more potent source of attack. The referees in South Africa allowed the side with possession to keep it under almost any circumstance. You could put in a great tackle, turning your man, and still not get the put-in even though you had wrapped the ball. We had not really prepared for this simply because you cannot. No matter how many discussions you might have with refs you never know until you are on the park just how they are going to behave. As we found out, you do not have to stay on your feet to retain the ball. So if the momentum slowed down, teams played for the scrum. A scrum, with the new law about the No.8 packing in the middle channel, is a better attacking option than slow ball.

We upped the pace considerably in the closing stages. Tony Underwood scored within three minutes of coming on as a substitute for Ieuan Evans. We had decided to use subs tactically throughout the tour. We had not

Tom Smith into early action against Eastern Province.

really come to terms with the concept during the northern hemisphere season. You have to weigh up whether a significant change in tactics or just a fresh pair of legs might be to your best advantage. The subs worked a treat for us here. Tony scored, Barry Williams, who had come on at the same time in place of Keith Wood, had a steaming run up the middle while Jeremy Davidson, who replaced Simon Shaw in the 72nd minute, was in a strike position three metres out but knocked on. It does not always work out as well as this.

Jerry Guscott and Will Greenwood rounded off a very satisfactory afternoon with two good tries. It had been a far from perfect exhibition but we had stuck to our guns. It would have been so easy for the players to have gone back into their shells when they trailed 11–10. They did not. They had the nerve and the belief to maintain a positive approach. There was plenty still to work on, which was very much the tenor of my conversation with Jim Telfer as we walked home from a Port Elizabeth restaurant late that night. The next day we moved on to East London. It was good to be under way.

There are always easy stereotypes floating about in rugby, so when you are short of a line you can pull one down and apply it to a player or a team. For the Lions the sweeping statement concerned the weather. We play through cold wet northern-hemisphere winters, so therefore we must all love cold wet weather. Furthermore it must suit our rugby. Nothing could be further from the truth. We would all prefer to play under clear skies and on firm grounds. The folk in East London did not appear to appreciate this. It rained hard and the winds blew throughout our four days there. The front page of the local paper captured the mood on the Monday. At the top right-hand side was a story headlined: 'Muddy Field Awaits the Lions'. Further down the page, tucked away, was a seemingly unimportant item: 'Assassination Plot Against Mandela Uncovered'. I think the placing of the two stories tells you something about people's priorities.

The change in the weather did not alter our focus at all. As a coach you are always on your toes in the early part of a tour, eager to see how players react to and relate to each other, how the mood of the squad is and what the possibilities are. It was obvious to me right from the start that this lot were serious about their business. If any proof were needed, then the Monday morning training session in East London proved it. It was not just that one of the early scrums blew up and Barry Williams and Mark Regan, the two hookers, traded punches. That was a trivial incident which inevitably grabbed the headlines. It illustrated to me just how passionate they were about their places. Of course if the niggle had carried on between the pair, and had festered off the pitch, then we would have stepped in and spoken to them both. As it was, they were chatting and laughing about it on the coach back from the ground.

It was not this minor spat which encouraged me to think we were on the right lines, it was the sense of shared purpose. It was a hard session. The Wednesday side were put through their paces on the main pitch. I do not think the groundsman was too happy with us because it cut up badly. In opposition, wearing padded tackle suits, was the team who had played against Eastern Province. They gave nothing away, crashing in as hard as possible. It was their contribution to the well-being of the whole squad, making sure that the Wednesday side got a good work-out, that impressed me. At the end of the 90-minute session the two sides applauded each other's efforts. It was spontaneous, but spoke volumes about how much respect there was for all concerned.

It was still wet by kick-off time on Wednesday against Border. A huge amount of surface water was standing on the pitch. There was a time when our players might have gone back into their shells at the prospect of playing in such conditions. There was no way that these Lions were going to revert to type. There is a myth which says that in wet weather you should kick. It is not true. The ball will get wetter the more often it hits the pitch. The best ball is the ball which goes through the hand. It gets drier the more often it is handled. You do have to trim your ambitions, but only in the sense that you pass shorter so as to retain control.

We were almost undone by our terrific start, John Bentley scoring after just two minutes. It was a great score which contained so many elements of play. There was a chip kick by Paul Grayson, a fast recycle, Tim Stimpson coming into the line well and a smart finish by Bentos. The ease of the try perhaps deluded us into thinking that it would all fall into place quite quickly. The type of game we were trying to play requires a high level of concentration. For the rest of that half we got distracted, tried to force the pace too much. We took the ball on too far at times which meant that the support was too far away when it was time to pass.

We trailed 11–10 just after half-time, but I was not too concerned. I decided to switch the focal point of attack by substituting Austin Healey with Matt Dawson. The conditions were not ideally suited to Austin's game. He is a runner and flick passer, whereas Matt is good at getting the forwards on the move and bringing in the midfield runners. I was aware, too, that Paul Grayson was out of sorts. I had toyed with the idea of substituting him, but opted instead to take the pressure off him by bringing on Matt. It worked. You could tell from the state of the pitch – brown and churned in their half, still green in ours – where the rugby was being played. We just were not putting away the chances. Finally we got it all together in the last twenty minutes. Rob Wainwright went over in

Rob Wainwright finally ploughs through the Border defence for a much-needed try.

For Scott Gibbs the end of the game against Border, but luckily the injury was not as serious as it first looked.

the 72nd minute after a good drive from the line out by Doddie Weir and Tim Stimpson made it safe with a last-minute penalty to give us an 18–14 victory.

It was not the most satisfying performance I had ever witnessed, but I did genuinely feel that there was a lot of good in it. We handled seventy times in the second half which is a decent return in any circumstances. We had started to get the runners into the right channels and worked the ball up the field with a good degree of patience. A defeat would have been a blow to morale.

There were a couple of injuries to worry about. Scott Gibbs had left the field just after

half-time in some considerable pain. From the sideline it looked like a bad ankle injury. The press boys were floating the notion that he might be the first casualty of the tour. My faith is always in medical diagnosis and in Dr James Robson we have one of the best. I had worked with James in 1993 and I have not known him to be wrong yet. He got Gavin Hastings onto the field on that tour and here he was optimistic that Scott might shape up all right too. Scott himself knew how to handle himself in such a situation. The ice went on immediately and he kept his leg up all evening. James and he went on the first flight down to Cape Town the next morning where they would see an orthopaedic surgeon. By the time we arrived there the following evening, James had figured that Scott would be on song within a week. He was proved right.

There was far more anxiety over Paul Grayson. He had struggled from an early stage against Border. It was not just that he was missing kicks, it was more that he was dropping back into the pocket, afraid to take the game on. It turned out that Paul had strained a muscle on Tuesday which he had now aggravated. It was a different injury to the one which had sidelined him back in England. James feared the worst. We decided to give it twenty-four hours, but already my mind was thinking about alternatives.

It was a very worrying time behind the scenes because Eric Miller and Tom Smith were also both struggling. Tom had injured his neck against Eastern Province and also had to go for a scan in Cape Town. It was a very painful injury but, as it turned out, an inconsequential one. Eric had what looked like a fractured cheekbone. His face had gone numb during the second half of the Border match. Again, he expected the worst. However the facilities in Cape Town were state of the art. They had an X-ray machine way beyond the norm. Eric's injury, which was damage to a very minor part of the face, would not have been spotted on an ordinary X-ray machine, and it was almost not picked up on this one either. There was a fault on the machine and it just happened that there was a technician in the building when the boys arrived. It was only a fuse which had blown and so Eric was soon being X-rayed. When the news came through soon afterwards that he had a minor problem, his face just erupted into smiles.

It is a major blow to everyone when a player has to go home. You can easily forget just how human, and how prone to ordinary emotions all the players are. It was quite distressing, therefore, to realise that someone I knew well, Paul Grayson, was on the plane home. We knew on Friday for sure that Paul had no chance of recovery. We decided to keep the news to ourselves. If we had released it then it would have upset the team preparing to play Western Province the day after. Fran was making a few preliminary phone calls, but we thought Sunday would be soon enough to confirm that Paul was heading back to England and that Mike Catt was on his way from Argentina. The fact that Mike was due to play the first Test for England in Argentina was another factor in our decision to delay the announcement.

As it was, we almost did not get him at all. Jack Rowell, the England manager, wanted Catt to stay on to play in the second Test for England the following Saturday. That was unacceptable. Mike had to be with us as soon as possible. Jack Rowell took some persuading. Mike could have left Buenos Aires that Sunday. Instead England flew to Mendoza which meant that Mike had to

fly back down again the next day. It was a waste of his time and of ours. The whole incident was threatening to become a major issue. For those two days we thought we were not going to get him. Fran had long phone calls with Bob Weighill, the secretary of the Home Unions, and directly with Jack Rowell in Argentina.

In the end Fran made it clear to Jack Rowell that if he did not make a firm decision about releasing Mike Catt then we would go elsewhere

Answering the Lions' call – Mike Catt leaves his hotel in Argentina.

for a replacement. Mike knew nothing about any of this which would have been a terrible state of affairs. Finally at 12.45 am on the Sunday, Fran made his last call. After twenty minutes he had to make it clear to Jack Rowell – 'Yes or no. Which is it?' It was obvious now that Jack had support from a couple of senior RFU figures. Fran asked for the phone to be passed over to Derek Morgan, chairman of the RFU playing committee. At the last gasp Derek Morgan sanctioned his release. It should never have happened. The Lions are by far the biggest thing to happen in British and Irish rugby. They have to take precedence over every other concern, otherwise they have no future.

So much for the drama surrounding Mike's arrival. Paul Grayson's departure was also an emotional experience. It is so tough for the player himself. He has arrived as part of a large group, but now has to get on the plane and go back on his own. We took Paul with us to Pretoria after the Western Province game from where he flew back. A couple of the players – Jeremy Guscott and Jason Leonard – took Paul out for a few drinks before he left. It seems a simple enough gesture, but it really does mean something to the player concerned. Those remaining obviously have to put an injury behind them as quickly as possible and get on with the tour. But they know, too, that it could be them. It was typical of this squad that they should spare a thought for Paul at the moment he most needed it.

That was all in the aftermath of the Western Province game. The arrival in Cape Town gave the whole squad a nice jolt. The pilot took us on a detour round Table Mountain on approach which was spectacular in itself, and then the sight of the Newlands stadium, which was just next door to the hotel in which we were staying, alerted everyone to the fact that it was now all for real from hereon in. Newlands is a major stadium, there was a full house of over 50,000 due and we would have to prove ourselves.

It was to be Martin Johnson's first game. It was a great day for him which I thought he handled well in his normal low-key but effective way. Newlands is a terrific ground to play on with the spectators all hemmed in so close. I think some modern stadiums have got it all wrong, Twickenham being a notable case in point. You are so far away from the action as a spectator that you never get really involved. The players become aware of that too. Newlands is the opposite. It has a superb atmosphere.

We went well against Western Province. They were a good side even if they'd slipped out of the Super 12. They had a very quick back three in Small, Swart and Berridge. We knew we would be asked a lot of questions. Our aim was still to show that British rugby could not be written off as slow, ponderous and predictable. That was why I was not too perturbed afterwards about the criticism of our tight scrummaging. We had not really worked at all on that aspect. What we had spent time on was the patterns of play all around the field. Within thirteen minutes we saw all that labour pay off again when John Bentley finished off an impressive sequence which went from a line out through several phases before Bentos was put clear. We were 13–0 up a few moments later when Tim Stimpson kicked a penalty. We could have been even further ahead but were just straining a bit too hard, running too far and getting isolated. Patience is not a virtue you learn overnight.

Our defence was strong. The attitude of the Rugby League boys helped. Alan Tait, Allan

Lawrence Dallaglio escapes the clutches of the Western Province defence to set up another attacking opportunity for the Lions. (Below) Richard Hill is stopped in his tracks as the Lions go on the offensive.

Bateman, Scott Gibbs and John Bentley know all about the importance of defending that gain line, of being offensive in the tackle. We had also done a lot of work on defensive patterns. I had noticed how the South Africans put a lot of ball back inside, using Honiball's strength to draw the defender across. We worked, therefore, on plugging the gap. The idea was for players to take a channel and to spread out across the field, almost like a Rugby League defence. As the play moves across the field it was our aim not just to drift across, but for the man furthest away to keep moving forward and across so that he would get into the space that the South

Africans wanted to attack if they put the ball back inside. Our players therefore worked in groups of three, making sure that one filled behind the ball-carrier but on a parallel, one attacked the ball-carrier and the other squeezed the space. We called it the scorpion's tail.

We needed to be strong defensively against Western Province because they came back at us. We held an early drive but then Muir went over after a lot of pressure. He scored again just before half-time to make it 14–18. We had got our second try in the 26th minute after some great passing from Jerry Guscott, Alan Tait and John Bentley – Alan eventually finishing it off. When Brink scored for Western Province early in the second half, we trailed 21–18. I know what we are capable of, however, so rarely panic. Sure enough we got stronger as the game went on with Ieuan Evans and John Bentley running in two tries in the last ten minutes to give us a 21–38 victory. It was hard fought which was good. We needed a big test, to see whether we could sustain our principles under pressure. You see so much about players' characters in such situations. We played with our backsides out to win the game. As Martin Johnson said afterwards, it was one of the fastest games he had ever played in. All our players stepped up a gear that afternoon.

And so to Pretoria. The fact that we would be at altitude (Johannesburg is about 5000ft above sea level, Pretoria a few hundred feet lower) did not affect us greatly. A few of the players found that their throats felt scorched and dry, but you quickly learn to play through it. In medical terms you either have to go in and out in a day or stay about eleven days to acclimatise completely. We were there for exactly eleven days which might have been shrewd planning by

the South Africans. It did not make any significant impact on us at all. The key thing is to drink a lot up there because, although it is winter, the sun can be deceptively strong.

Every Sunday night we had a coaching meeting where we appraised the week before and set our objectives for the week coming up. Jim Telfer and I made up the principal coaching team. Jim and I go back a long way, working together most recently in the Scottish Grand Slam set-up in 1990. We are on the same wavelength when it comes to rugby. He believes very firmly in having strong characters in a side, guys you can trust in a tight corner to make the right decisions and not to buckle under pressure. Jim is a harder taskmaster than I am, but it is a front in some ways. He pushes players hard, but only because it brings the best out of them. They would not want it any other way. Jim has got a great sense of humour, too, and is always keen to listen to players. It was clear that we both had enormous respect for this group.

You only had to talk to Jim after a Monday morning session on the back pitch at Loftus Versfeld to appreciate that. Jim really put the forwards through it, especially the Wednesday side. They did 45 scrums in 42 minutes, but never once complained. That is what Jim calls an honest type of player, one you know will not let his mates down. We had always known that there would come a point when we had to work on the tight scrum. This was the time. Not that we were deficient in either technique or poundage, it was more that we had to get timing and co-ordination right.

There were other important members of the coaching panel – Dave Alred, the kicking coach, and Andy Keast, the technical advisor. Andy, who was out at Natal for a couple of years before moving to Harlequins to team up with Dick Best, put in an enormous amount of work in the early part of the tour. It was also pretty unglamorous labour, holed up a darkened room peering at a computer screen. What he did though was so important for us. Using computer software which had been used extensively in Australian Rules football, Andy was able to dissect a game completely for us. With the technical assistance of Ian Brunning from Castle Sport and Leisure, who manufactured the equipment, Andy would programme the computer to record and isolate different aspects of the game – the line out, for example – or the tackling of a particular player or, perhaps, the defensive alignment of a side. It called for hours and hours of study and Andy would frequently be working way past midnight. By the end of it all, though, each player would have an individual videotape which he could take away and study. The tapes from the Western Province game showed us that we were on the right lines. We were keeping our shape well, attacking in waves and not getting flat or one-dimensional.

We thought that the test against Mpumalanga would be different. Everyone kept telling us that we would be in for a tough time up front. They had drawn with the All Blacks the previous year and put over 40 points on Wales before that. The province is about an hour's drive east of Pretoria, in farming and coal-mining country. We expected a very physical game, especially as they had drafted in some Northern Transvaal players to boost the squad, which had reached the Currie Cup quarter-finals and the semi-finals of the Nite Series. Well, it was a hard afternoon all right, but not in the way anticipated.

We played superb rugby and effectively had the game won within 18 minutes by which time we were 21–0 up, thanks to three tries from Rob Wainwright. We hit the groove from the kick-off, changing angles and supporting in depth. They did not actually miss many tackles, but we were

Ieuan Evans races through the Pumas defence on his way to scoring the first of his two tries.

tight and fluid. The passing out of the tackle was superb, particularly for Rob's second try. Up front we had them after 20 minutes. The front row said they looked them in the eyes and could tell they were gone. Their much-vaunted pack came off a distinct second-best. Maybe that was the reason for the assault on Doddie Weir. Or maybe it was just that their second row, Marius

Bosman, is a thug. He was at it all game. Their coach had even tipped off the Sky commentary team beforehand, saying that Bosman could be a decent player if only he learned to discipline himself.

Players like him should be drummed out of the sport. It is a hard enough game as it is without having to worry whether someone is

The stamping incident which left Doddie Weir's tour in tatters. Marius Bosman (inset) was later fined by the **SARFU**, but that seemed scant punishment in the eyes of the Lions management team.

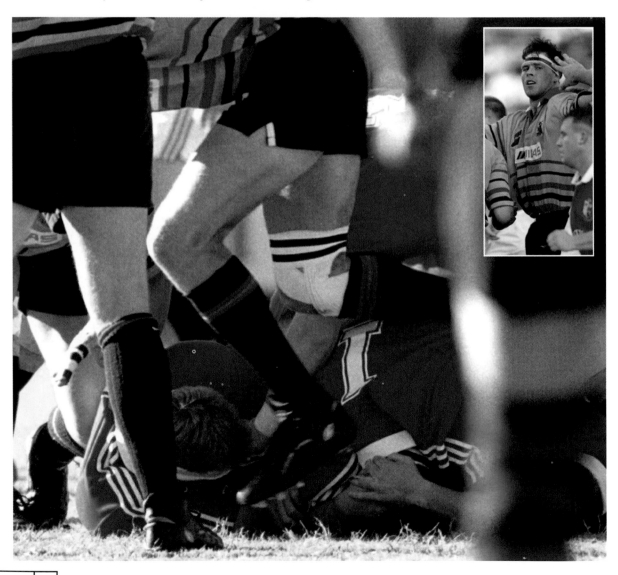

Tim Rodber rampages through the Mpumalanga defence. Attack for the Lions was the best possible retaliation for the Bosman incident.

going to maim you or not. I have played at every level and coached at it as well, and people like Bosman are not hard players. They are cheap, cowardly sorts at heart, unable to play the game properly and so resort to underhand shots as a result. Bosman could not make a mark on the field as a player, so he made one as a thug. He was a total idiot and I could not have blamed our players if they had taken the law into their own hands to sort him out. They did not, perhaps because they did not realise themselves until afterwards quite what Bosman had done.

Early in the second half he stamped on Doddie's trapped leg, right on the cruciate ligament knee joint. It was deliberate and gratuitous. We later counted eight separate incidents on the

video in which he had either been punching, kicking or headbutting. The referee saw him stamp on Doddie, but unfortunately chose only to award a penalty – I cannot for the life of me understand why.

The result was that we could not cite Bosman for the incident. Under Super 12 and Tri-Nations regulations, a team can cite a player even if the matter has been dealt with by a referee. Under IB rulings you cannot. It is a nonsense and the IB have to standardise it. We could only appeal to the local union to take a stand, which they eventually did – fining Bosman R10,000, about £1,250. It was a hopelessly inadequate action. We are a touring side and SARFU should have stepped in. Bosman should have been banned for at least a year. Doddie may be out for that long. Why should Bosman not suffer likewise? Fining is a cop-out and sends out all the wrong signals. Mpumalanga should be ashamed of themselves. Bosman is a coward and has no place on a rugby field. He was an animal and I was very, very angry. The other second row, Elandre van den Berg, was not an awful lot better.

Doddie had been in tremendous form and was a real contender for a Test place. He even played on for a few minutes after the incident, which tells you something about the size of his heart. But James Robson knew it was serious as soon as he saw it. The scan the next day confirmed our fears and Doddie was off the tour. It put a blight on what was an outstanding performance, to win 64–14 and play very stylish rugby. It was the perfect preparation for the trial of the 'Big Three' which lay ahead.

Doddie Weir was left on crutches, out of the tour and possibly out of the game for up to a year. For Marius Bosman – a fine of £1,250.

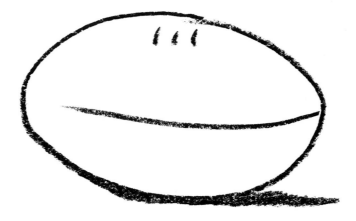

ON THE BALL
IN THE WORLD
OF FINANCIAL
SERVICES

HSBC

A WORLD OF FINANCIAL SERVICES

Issued by HSBC Holdings plc, 10 Lower Thames Street, London EC3R 6AE, United Kingdom.

3. THE BIG THREE

It was one hell of a proposition. This was the make-or-break part of the tour. There is no country in the world which would have fancied our itinerary. To play Northern Transvaal, Gauteng (Transvaaal) and Natal within eight days is an enormous task. Potentially it could have been a lethal assignment. In theory we could have lost all three. It would have been so difficult to salvage the tour if that had happened. Morale and self-belief are very fragile qualities which need the succour of victory to keep them alive.

I do not buy into the notion that the ride was that much easier because the Springbok coach Carel du Plessis had withdrawn his players from their respective provincial teams. Those players might have made a difference, but who really knows? They might have held back for fear of injury or their replacements might have seen it as a golden opportunity to make a real mark. In South Africa, too, the strength in depth is considerable. If the locals do not think it is so, then they should try playing in Scotland where we really do have to make the best of what we have got. There are good players at every level in South Africa, of that there is no doubt.

There was no fixed selection policy coming into these games, no intention to settle on Test combinations as soon as possible so as to give them optimum time together. All we were concerned about was giving everyone a chance to show what they could do against a Super 12 side. We still wanted to try out different options which is why we put Eric Miller on the open side against Northern Transvaal. Richard Hill had a slight calf injury so it was an ideal opportunity to see if Eric could transfer his dynamic play at No.8 across to the open side.

In retrospect it did not prove an awful lot in that the back row were under so much pressure in the scrums that they spent most of the game on the back foot. As a result we found it very difficult to build the platforms for the backs we thought we might be able to do. As for people saying it was a mistake trying Eric at No.7, I just do not agree. If you think a player has something to offer then you have got to find out for real. Eric is a tremendously hard worker, very forceful with the ball in hand and an excellent footballer. But, at the moment, he is a better No.8 than he is a No.7, which is what we found out from that game. The selection

The game against Northern Transvaal provided the opportunity to try Eric Miller at No.7.

told us something and therefore was vindicated.

It was a tough game against Northern Transvaal. For the first half an hour we did not play at all. In fact it was the worst thirty minutes on tour. We thought we could do it without putting in the hard work. We were going through the motions, thinking that it would all come right as it had done against Mpumalanga and Eastern Province. In short, we thought we were better than we actually were at this stage of the tour. There is nothing like the stark experience itself for bringing a message home. We had told them often enough that if you try to take short-cuts against South African sides, that if you lose your focus and neglect the basics, then they will swarm all over you. That is what happened in that opening half hour. Northerns played all the football, taking the game to us and executing their scores well. We knew that we would get a testing up front and so it proved. The tight five had a bad day at the office.

The heartening thing for me was that the players themselves realised what was going on and were in the process of rectifying it for

Things certainly were not going to plan for Ian McGeechan and Jim Telfer against Northern Transvaal. A try in the first minute of the second half left the Lions trailing 25–7.

themselves by half-time. With the longer break (ten minutes) there is more scope to run over events. I did not lay into them at all. There is no point and it is not my style. All you do is to highlight certain areas which need addressing. In essence we needed to become tighter so that we could play more loosely and freely. We had to concentrate more, cement the tight scrum so as to allow our continuity to develop. By the end we had manufactured some very good tries by doing just that – putting players into holes and following them through. That was the gist of the half-time exchanges. We were only 18–7 down – Jerry had fashioned one of his specials, a chip over a flat defence with wonderful timing on the pick-up for the try – and were still very much in the hunt. The last thing that Jim Telfer said as we left the field at half-time was that if they were to score next it would become an impossible task.

They scored next. It was a soft try just fifty seconds after the restart which again came from one of our weak areas of play on the day, the scrum. It is such a key part of the game now, one which we had not quite come to terms with. The switch in emphasis, from line out to scrum, had not happened in the northern hemisphere simply because the law changes had not taken effect there yet. Now that the No.8 has to pack down at all times there is so much more scope for attacking from the base. The result is that you want to keep the ball on the field more, either to retain or recycle possession or to force the scrum. So there is less kicking to touch and far more emphasis on keeping the ball in hand and working downfield. I think we might have swung too far the other way in our desire to see continuity. You have to have a fair contest for the ball and if the tackler has done his job and forced his man up and back to your side then you should win the put-in. Instead, in several games here, we were thwarted time and again as the opposition got the put-in. The scrum was just so much more significant than the line out. We had twelve throw-ins from touch in one

Rob Wainwright leads the charge, backed-up by Jeremy Guscott and Lawrence Dallaglio as the Lions try to fend off the first defeat of the tour.

match against more than thirty scrums. I would prefer to see a more even split.

The scrum and the line out are totally different phases. The scrum will also give you two sides of the field to play with. It also means that you have got sixteen forwards packed into a small area of the field who have got to stay there until the scrum half releases the ball. If you are able to exploit the tight head, come up on the right shoulder and swivel the back row away, then there is very little the other side can do to defend. That is how Richter scored that critical try just after half-time for Northern Transvaal.

We had done a lot of work that week on our scrummaging but there was still more to do. It was a question of getting the collective timing right and of adapting to the way the scrum is refereed there. They come from further away, the hit is that much bigger and they keep pushing on contact. If you do not meet it right then you lose ground immediately. We were still scrumming too high which played into their hands. It was a gradual process of refinement. By the first Test we had got it right. We aimed to get in low, to shuffle half a pace across just before impact so as to come up on their left or right shoulder. They did not like it at all. If you watch the tapes you see how often they drop the scrum if they are not happy. Natal, for example, kept on going to the floor

There was a lot of talk about us selecting mobile, ball-handling forwards, men such as Tom Smith and Paul Wallace. Jim Telfer and I were adamant that you could not select a player in that position on his footballing ability alone. First and foremost he had to be able to scrummage. You cannot even begin to consider his input round the field if he has not done the business for you in the tight. We had real pressure for places too, so we could have selected any one of three or four combinations. Those that did win Test places did so because they were able to do everything.

Northern Transvaal was a watershed game for us. We trailed 25–7 with most of the second half still to play. Yet we did not panic or throw the towel in. We carved out some very good scores, playing at pace and with vision. Gregor Townsend made a wonderful break for Jerry Guscott's second try of the game four minutes into the second half. I had never had any doubts at all about Gregor's ability. He had had a

Gregor Townsend powers through the Northern Transvaal defence to create a try for Jeremy Guscott and keep the Lions in the game.

difficult season but only because so much was heaped upon him. The only game he started as fly half for Scotland was against England. His forwards won only 27 per cent of the ball in that game. It was asking for a miracle to get him to do something from that. Gregor's confidence

Lawrence Dallaglio checks for
support as his progress is stopped.

had taken a blow during the season. He is an outstanding talent. It was my role to give that talent the opportunity to come out, to express itself and in so doing liberate other players around him. Even though Gregor had a free rein we did also impress upon him the importance of collective responsibility, that he could not be too loose and that there could not be too many slack passes. One here against Northern Transvaal let van Schalkwyk in for a try. That made the score 32–20, just as we were beginning to work our way back into it. Gregor made some amends with his try five minutes before the end, again showing his speed and eye for space to take him clear.

But we had lost, 35–30, and it was a serious point of the tour. It was the first real test of the attitude in the squad. When you are winning, it is easy to get on well. When you lose, those relationships can come under strain. When we got back to the hotel in Pretoria, I took the whole squad to the team room for a five-minute chat. I told them that they were still in my opinion a very special bunch of players and that I still truly believed that they had the ability to go all the way in the Test series. I had not said that to them much on tour before but I just wanted them to know how I felt that evening, that I still had faith in them all and in our mission. If they were what I thought they were, then the experience of defeat would make them stronger. The way they reacted to the defeat, and the way they trained the next morning, would determine how good a touring party we really were.

It was a good brisk session the next morning. You felt already that lessons were being absorbed, that all the players, even those who were only in rehabilitation training at the Health and Racquets Club, had narrowed their focus, knowing that we were in a crunch few days. I had told them that if we could just accept that there was never going to be an easy period in a game, never mind an easy game, then we would be able to cope with anything. Commitment was a key concept. Our game might look loose and fluid but it actually demands a tremendous level of concentration and input of energy.

That Sunday was officially a rest day even though we did some work. It was only the second day off for the players. There was an unwelcome interruption to the morning's programme when Fran had to go with Scott Gibbs to a disciplinary tribunal at Loftus Versfeld. Scott had been cited for what they deemed to be a punch thrown in the tackle. We took the panel's verdict which was a one-match ban. In my opinion the action should never have been taken. It was small-minded and left a nasty feeling. There is little doubt that it was someone – I have no idea who – just getting in his twopennyworth after we had quite rightly made such a fuss about the attack on Doddie a few days before. The two incidents were completely different. Doddie's was a brutal assault, Scott's a questionable, borderline all-enveloping tackle. There was no need to cite.

We could not afford to get distracted from our main goal, however. This is where Fran handles things well. We decided to take it on the chin and move on. With Doddie we felt we owed it to him to make a very strong and sustained protest, which we did. It is so easy on a tour to get irritated by things. You have not got time to do so. Fran and I both told Scott that nothing would be held against him. His tour fees would not be affected nor, more crucially, would his chances of a Test place. He would still be very much in the frame for selection.

On the Monday afternoon we held a clinic in Soweto. It was a very arresting experience. We have done clinics in different townships down the years but this was different. The very name itself conjures up sharp images: of trouble and hardship and violence and poverty. It made you appreciate the reality of the place when the police on our coach strapped on their guns as they got off. Actually to have a chance to go in and see for yourself – admittedly no more than a snapshot – was quite uplifting. People are struggling by, somehow or other, in this vast, sprawling place. There was rubbish everywhere yet real signs of ordinary life. I know these

clinics are cosmetic but from our point of view they can't be anything else. We had a small window of time and were happy to give it over if we could. On top of that we were directed by SARFU as to where we should go. I hope the kids we saw got something out of it. Certainly they seemed more established rugby players than normal, with some of them having real potential. Let us hope they get a few breaks to help them make it.

There is so little opportunity to go off-track these days on a tour. Some might think it sad and I am sure that we might even have come in for a bit of criticism in some quarters, but there is absolutely no other way of doing it. It is all so different from previous tours where you could unwind for a few days, really let your hair down

Lawrence Dallaglio leads by example as the Lions hold a coaching clinic in Soweto – one of the rare excursions on tour.

and go into the community wherever you happened to be. Now that everyone is paid, then rugby is the only real priority. We would soon get flak if we were spending half our week on safari.

The players themselves adapted well, particularly on this tour. The League boys were

that we did not waste their time. On previous tours there had been a lot of unnecessary meetings, talking about what you were going to do rather than just going out there and doing it. We would have a five-minute chat before training and that was it.

I also made a point of involving the senior

Back to business for the Lions as they prepare for another training session.

a help in that regard. They are used to clocking on and clocking off. The fitness levels required to play the modern game mean there is so little slack in the system. The boys often trained twice a day and then, of course, had to recuperate. What I tried to do was make sure

players more on this tour. In that way there could be a constant feedback of information and ideas between both sides. We wanted a flat management structure with few hierarchies. The players we brought in were Martin Johnson, obviously, Tim Rodber, Ieuan Evans, Jeremy

Guscott, Lawrence Dallaglio, Rob Wainwright and Keith Wood. They all have enormous experience and it would be madness not to use them. It was not just a means of saving time by avoiding meetings. All these players had a direct say in the tactics, the strategy and the approach. I like to think that part of the reason we had a good squad ethos was that we treated players with respect and accorded them responsibility.

The Gauteng game was now make-or-break. We couldn't take two defeats in a row. It would have crippled the momentum of the whole tour. The two replacements, Mike Catt and Nigel Redman, were due their first games. I had been very impressed with both of them. Mike had been so close to selection in the first place that it was great to see him get the opportunity. He fitted in superbly from the very moment he arrived. He got to South Africa just before the Mpumalanga game. That evening we had a scheduled session back in Pretoria, an hour's

Nigel Redman, one of the game's great soldiers. It was great to have him on board.

drive away. Mike was zonked from travelling across time zones and also had a slight groin problem. But he trained. He wanted to be part of it as soon as he could.

Ollie Redman is one of the game's great soldiers. It was absolutely marvellous to see him with us. As he himself knew and admitted only too readily, he was not the first-choice replacement. He gave one of the funniest press conferences I have ever heard just after teaming up with us in Pretoria. He is so honest, sincere and down-to-earth. He was asked how the news was broken to him that he was to join the Lions from the England tour in Argentina.

'I got a call from Jack Rowell in the hotel to come round to his room,' said Ollie. 'I assumed he was going to tell me that I was dropped. When he said that I was going to South Africa I said, "I don't believe it." "Neither do I," said Jack Rowell.'

Mike Catt in training for his first game as a Lion against Gauteng.

Anyway it was good to have them on board. Both players would offer us so much through their play and their attitude. They were keen to show what they had to offer against Gauteng. They were both involved in a heavy contact session we had on the Monday. We all knew we had to find the intensity we lacked against Northern Transvaal. The two props chosen were Tom Smith and Paul Wallace. I was keen to see how they would go. They had done so well against Mpumalanga. Now was to be an even bigger test. They were not packing quite the same pressure on our scrum machine as some of the others, but in the actual live scrums, such as the week before, they were tight and co-ordinated. They took on Mpumpalanga and the game was over after twenty minutes.

We had a brief session under the Loftus lights on the Tuesday before the match. Floodlights take a bit of getting used to. The ball tends to come at you a little quicker, particularly over the last twenty feet or so. It is just because you do not have the same depth of field at night. There is also more dew on the ground which means you have to be adjust accordingly. We kicked off at different times throughout the tour: 3.15, 7.15 (as here) and 5.15 for the Test matches. It was all done to suit television and I have absolutely no problem with that. We are in a professional era and if we want to get revenue into the game then we have to accept the consequences. As long as it does not get silly, I do not see any problem. All we need to do from our point of view is to stagger the build-up to suit the kick-off time. You do exactly the same activities but just change the hour.

I presented the Lions jerseys to Mike Catt and Ollie Redman in the dressing-room just before kick-off. It is always a special moment.

The game itself went as we expected. We knew they would be tough. They had not been as badly affected as other provinces by the withdrawals for the Springboks. Both Hennie le Roux and Kobus Wiese were playing. Sure enough, the opening was torrid. We survived it, although we had that little bit of luck that all touring teams hope for when Hendricks knocked on in the early stages with a clear run to the line. Our defence was such an integral part of our game, so crucial to our self-belief.

Barry Williams and Chris Rossouw get better acquainted during the clash with Gauteng. The Lions were under no illusions that this would be an easy game.

The fact that we survived those first fifteen minutes set the tone for the rest of the tour. Here we were under the cosh and coping. They were playing typical South African rugby – hard, direct and powerful. Even though we were 9–3 down at the break, we had nothing to be afraid of. Our defence could cope with anything, I felt.

We had put in a lot of work on the training field to get it right. Every session we did always contained some sort of defensive drill, anything from five minutes to fifty. Against Northern Transvaal we had been careless in midfield. We had also been guilty of getting too tight in the rucks and mauls. We needed to fill into the channels and widen our defence so that one long pass could not beat our defensive line.

In the second half it was our attack which really made an impression. The Austin Healey try in the 63rd minute epitomised what we were trying to achieve. We had to be patient to make it all work. If we rushed it, snatched at the passes or went too far, then it would fall apart. Here we were patient and, sure enough, it all came to pass. Although Austin caught the eye at the death with a great angled sprint to the line it was the long build-up which was really significant. We went through about seven phases – from line out to drive to midfield recycle to a fringe attack down the blind side and lots of passing out of tackles. Suddenly there was a glint of light and Austin went for it, finishing off a sequence lasting 1 minute 48 seconds.

We still trailed 9–8. Neil Jenkins, though, had come on as a replacement not long after half time. Mike Catt had been goal-kicking up to that point. He had been on duty for England in Argentina and done well so we went with him here. It was too much of a call for him perhaps,

Touchdown for Austin Healey as he finishes off a magnificent Lions move – things were starting to come together.

having only just found his feet in South Africa. He only hit one from six chances. Neil came on and within five minutes was stroking the conversion over from the touchline to put us in the lead at 10–9. To me it was one of the defining moments of the tour. To score such a good try and then turn it into maximum points really showed that we meant business. To land a conversion like that gives such a psychological boost to one side and deflates the other. It was quite simply why Neil was on tour. He was a very good footballer in his own right too, better than people give him credit for, as he showed against Mpumalanga. It was that game which settled my concerns that Neil might not have got it all back after his long lay-off with injury. In the first match against Eastern Province he had looked out of sorts. Now he was playing without any thought for his injured arm and was back to his best.

Our second try four minutes later was a wonder try by John Bentley. He picked the ball up inside our half and then set off down the right touchline, outside a couple of Gauteng players and then cutting inside three more. He must have covered 75 metres in all. He had a chance to pass inside to Jerry Guscott at one point but kept heading for the line instead. It

was pure Bentos. He makes mistakes at times but he does make things happen around him.

To win at Ellis Park was a huge scalp for us. We were in among the big boys, on their own patch, taking all that they could throw at us and winning. The longer the game went on the more pedestrian they looked. We might have had another couple of scores and certainly one try when Jerry Guscott and Mike Catt did not click after a great break. It was a certain try if the pass had not been knocked on. Neil Back had a terrific evening. Jim Telfer and I had been very keen to get him on tour. There was no good setting out to play the way we did if we did not have the right link men. Neil fitted the bill

Neil Back bursts through the Gauteng defence during yet another polished performance.

Rob Wainwright threatens the Gauteng defence.

perfectly. He gave us a different dimension in that he was in and out of contact so quickly that the ball was flowing just as we wanted it to do. Neil has got great upper body strength, particularly for a man of his size, and is the equal of most of the other forwards. It is his awareness of play unfolding, and his ability to get there, which really tells.

The whole squad knew how big a win that was for us. They all, down to the last man of the back-up, made their way down to the dressing-room to applaud the team in. It was a genuine show of support for their efforts and what they had done for the tour. It made me realise just how strong a group we were collectively.

We had dinner in a room provided by Dr Louis Luyt, which meant that we did not have to mix in with the main reception and be unable to eat until very late, and also perhaps not get the food we needed. The opposition were there and we had a good evening.

We left Pretoria on Thursday afternoon to head back down to the coast in Durban. It is always good to be in one place for a decent amount of time on tour. We had had eleven days in Pretoria which meant that we could get the suitcases unpacked and really unwind. There was not that much on offer in Pretoria in the immediate vicinity, so the boys got through a lot of films. We had taken advice about security before coming out and the view was that we did not need a permanent police escort. England did in 1994, as did the All Blacks in 1996. We felt that it was not necessary and that the players themselves would just be sensible. Tom Smith had a habit of wandering off for long walks by himself but even he did not stray too far off the beaten track. While the need for caution is paramount in a country like South Africa, you cannot confine the players to barracks all the time or they would go stir crazy. They need to have their own space on occasions.

After the Gauteng win the whole squad was buzzing. The Thursday morning session before we left for Durban was an absolute cracker. You could feel the edge and the energy. We were on a roll and we knew it. We flew down in the afternoon and landed in torrential rain. There were a few of poor flyers in the party – James Robson, the doctor, and Sam Peters, the administrative secretary are just two – so they were not too at ease during the one-hour flight.

Then we were back to where we started from, the Beverly Hills Hotel at Umhlanga Rocks, right on the Indian Ocean and about a quarter of an hour's drive from Durban. Some thought the backdrop was too comfortable and enticing, that it might distract us from our goal. It would take more than a beach hotel to deflect our squad from the task in hand. Their focus never once wavered. There is also no reason at all why they should have to put up with spartan surroundings just to get them in the mood. The hotels on the whole trip were good. Fran Cotton and Bob Weighill had done a reconnoissance trip back in the winter and worked out what would best suit our schedule and needs. All the hotels had excellent team rooms, well stocked with food, fruit and drinks as well as pool tables, darts and table tennis. It was important for the players to have somewhere in which they could just relax, get to know each other better and not mope around in their hotel bedrooms.

The Natal game was the last of the big three. It, too, was going to be a huge challenge. Natal were Currie Cup champions and had recently got to the semi-finals of the Super 12. Our technical advisor, Andy Keast's previous experience in South Africa worked to our advantage. All his contacts told him that Natal were out to show that they were the dominant province in South Africa and were hell-bent on using this game as a platform for showing the strength of Natal rugby.

Before we left the UK I thought we would be fielding a shadow Test team in this fixture. It was the players who made me change my mind. Their form, their commitment and their ability to make me sit up and take notice just kept me reviewing opinions and policy. The competition for places, and from unexpected quarters, was without doubt one of the principal strengths of the tour. We did not once put out the same XV in the build-up to the Test. What we had were any number of combinations which we could mesh together as we saw fit in any game and for any reason. We had intended not to have definite, defined Wednesday and Saturday sides as a matter of policy. However, you know that sometimes you have to trim your ideals accordingly. Here we never did and that is to the enormous and lasting credit of the entire squad. There was not one bad apple in the bunch.

We wanted to see how Tom Smith would go with Martin Johnson behind him in the scrum so Tom was to play for the second time that week. The midfield had proved to be a difficult selection area in that we were rarely able to play our original choice. Scott Gibbs had an early injury as had Allan Bateman who was troubled by a hamstring strain, an injury which

connections. We had studied their performances too in the Super 12. They had a reputation as the most fluid of South African teams so we had to make sure that we did not give them any room. They also had the best

Scott Gibbs was keen to make an impression following an early-tour injury and a one-match ban.

ultimately was to thwart his chances of making a real bid for a Test place. He just did not get enough rugby under his belt and this was a great shame as he was playing superbly.

We knew more about Natal than any other side if only because of Andy Keast's

goal-kicker in South Africa in their ranks, Gavin Lawless, so it was imperative not to give away penalties. If you do, and the kicker bangs them over, a side can quickly build momentum. We had planned to bottle up their scrum half, Kevin Putt, who could be a threat. As it was, he pulled out. The whole idea in studying the opposition is just to make your own players aware of certain patterns. You cannot be too rigid or dogmatic because if the opposition do not conform to type then you are caught cold. You work by impressions and respond to different trigger points. We knew too that the scrummage would once again be an area of pressure. Their hooker, John Allan, who I knew from Scotland days, was playing his last game for Natal before taking up a coaching post at London Scottish. He had two Springboks, Kempson and le Roux, on either side of him.

We made a great start, stringing together good passages of play right from the kick-off. We were then rocked by an injury to Robert Howley. Rob made a typical thrust in the sixth minute and fell awkwardly. He played on thinking it was just a bang but five minutes later had to come off. We were in radio contact with James Robson, the doctor. The immediate word from the field was that it was not too serious. As soon as James had a good look at him in the dressing-room, however, he realised that Rob's tour was over. He had dislocated his shoulder and would need an operation. It was such a shame for Rob who is a smashing lad and a wonderful player. He was having an immense tour. He suited our style perfectly with his powerful breaks, intelligent reading of the game and ability to bring the best out of all those around him.

The scrum halves in the party all had similar qualities, even though there were stylistic differences. Matt Dawson came on and did very well. We have said it so often but it still remains true – in sport you have to grab that opportunity when it comes by.

We were putting them under a lot of pressure and preventing them from getting any sort of momentum at all. More than in any other game we felt we had control right from the outset. We were good at reading the situation in this game. When they tried to push up hard and flat on us we chipped over. Keith Wood's chip in the 23rd minute caught them napping and allowed Gregor to score. Lawless kept them in the hunt with three penalties but at 16–9 at half-time I knew that we had them on the rack if we could step up our pace and intensity in the second half. We did. Neil Jenkins kicked four goals to

Gregor Townsend goes for touch watched closely by captain Martin Johnson.

keep the scoreboard on the move before we finished in style with two tries. Gregor chipped through for Mike Catt to score and then Lawrence Dallaglio rounded it all off with a great try in the last minute.

To me that try summed up so much of what we were about. Lawrence, like all the players, was very tired by this stage. He could easily have taken a second or two longer to get up from the breakdown. But he did not. He got back to the play, trailed the ball, the South Africans did not pick him up and he was through. The try proved that we were prepared to play to the nth degree no matter how badly or fatigued we felt. At home we had been used to living in the comfort zone at this stage of the match, looking for the softer options in order to run the clock down. These players were different. They were so committed to our whole ethos and playing philosophy that they did not think twice about looking for the easy way out. This meant that the level of involvement around the field was dispersed more equitably. Instead of having maybe seven or eight players doing all the donkey work, now it was all fifteen and so the principal players were in fact doing less.

The anguish shows on the face of Rob Howley as he realises that his tour is over.

We finished nearly every game on tour the stronger. People assumed we must have done lots of work on our fitness. Not at all. Dave McLean, our fitness advisor, monitored their levels, but there was no specific targeting of fitness at all. What happened was that the nature of our approach, with the ball in hand for a lot of each training session, meant that a lot of ground was being covered. They were fitness sessions in their own right. More than that was the commitment of the players to the game plan. They all had absolute trust in each other, a total belief that each of them would be there if needed. There was simply no question that any of them would not get off the deck that tiny bit more quickly in order to hit the support space he was supposed to fill. It was attitude which made us fit.

At the end of these demanding seven days I was very happy. We had responded magnificently to the Northern Transvaal defeat and were now in good order. The combinations were all knitting, the players all getting used to reading each other's body language around the field, a crucial asset when you are trying to play a fluid game. As we headed to Cape Town and the first Test, I could not have been in a better mood. We were ready for the Springboks.

Simon Shaw tries to power his way through the Natal defence as the forwards take control in an impressive victory. Next in line – the Springboks.

WE HAVE MAJOR PLAYERS IN OUR TEAM

HongkongBank

Midland Bank

Hang Seng Bank

Marine Midland Bank

Hongkong Bank of Canada

Banco HSBC Bamerindus

Hongkong Bank Malaysia

The British Bank of the Middle East

HongkongBank of Australia

HSBC Investment Banking

The HSBC Group

Over 5,000 offices in 78 countries

HSBC

A WORLD OF FINANCIAL SERVICES

Issued by HSBC Holdings plc, 10 Lower Thames Street, London EC3R 6AE, United Kingdom.

Surpass all the competition

Whether you're doing business internationally, nationally or locally, don't get lost in the scrum. Let KPMG keep their eye on the ball.

From tax advice to pensions, corporate finance deals to owner managed business advice. Call:

Richard Boot
Birmingham
0121 232 3000

David Murrell
London
0171 311 1000

KPMG
means business

4. THE FIRST TEST

There is nothing like the build-up to a Test match. All the preamble, all the talk is over. You can feel the players putting in that extra bit of effort, sense the tightening of the focus and then sniff a bit of tension in the air. It is what we are all in the game for – gearing ourselves up to face the big challenges. There are some people who go on about the pressure of it all. Well, if there were no pressure it would not be worth doing. It is because the occasion is huge, the outside scrutiny intense and the importance of victory so acute that you put in all that effort in the first place.

We arrived in Cape Town on Sunday evening and went almost straight into our weekly management meeting. Before we left the UK we had a campaign plan. Every week we revised it, amended it hugely or not at all, and really thrashed out just what we wanted to achieve that particular week. We would work out too just how many sessions we might have, and what sort of work we would concentrate on.

That Sunday we felt we were in a position of strength even though we still did not know our Test team. This was not a flaw, as was suggested in some quarters. I saw it as very much a positive thing. The game on Tuesday against the Emerging Springboks was still a live selection match. We wanted to see how Jeremy Davidson would go, for example. Obviously we settled on certain combinations. The half backs would be Matt Dawson and Gregor Townsend and we had decided that we definitely needed Neil Jenkins kicking at full back. We were not wholly decided on the centre combination. Jerry Guscott was playing so well at centre that it would have been

difficult, and unfair on him, to pick him on the wing. We wanted to see how Allan Bateman and he would work out as a centre pairing but because of Allan's injury problems never got the chance. In the end Allan was the unluckiest player of all to miss out on a Test spot because he did play some fabulous rugby.

These were all issues still to be resolved at our Tuesday night selection meeting. On Sunday we just planned the programme. We wanted to get out of town and break up the week for the players so we had fixed to go to Stellenbosch on the Wednesday, about an hour's drive from Cape Town up in wine-growing country. We'd been invited to lunch there but we also planned two sessions either side of lunch. By then the Test team would be known. We decided that the players would receive a letter under their doors at 8 o'clock that

Former Springbok, Jannie Engelbrecht, owner of one of the many wineries in the Stellenbosch region.

morning either congratulating them on making the twenty-one or commiserating with them. The first thing we did thereafter was to get them to meet up in the six small groups which we had set up back in Weybridge to thrash out just how they all felt about their own situation and how they would deal with it. From that half-hour discussion came the resolve of the non-Test players to bury their own disappointment and help the cause in any way they could. The support of those guys was crucial to the morale of the whole party. Our eventual series victory was a victory for the whole party not just for the players on the field. You will not find one person who would disagree with that.

The Emerging Springbok game was important, then, for selection but again also for morale. This was the first time we would be playing a Springbok jersey and if we could do some damage to the green and gold, it would fine-tune our sense of confidence. The weather was a bit troublesome with a lot of storms about. We started the game so well. In fact if we had to produce a video of what we were all about, then we could do no worse than package the first try which ended with almost the entire team in an unfamiliar position. The last two players in the ruck were half backs, Ollie Redman was at scrum-half and then it finally went through Ronnie Regan and Graham

Graham Rowntree goes over for the Lions' first try and finishes a marvallous passage of total rugby.

Rowntree on the outside. It was first-class, players playing the game without regard to the number on their back.

Another bit of magic from John Bentley provides the springboard for a grandstand finish.

After that we got casual. They closed the gap accordingly but, as we had seen before on tour, our boys had the self-belief and patience to wait for it to come back together. It did. We defended our line really well at one stage and then flicked a switch. Bentos took it up through the middle in his usual distinctive style and suddenly the whole fabric of the game changed. In the space of seven minutes we had everything. We got better and better and ran out comfortable and convincing winners. It was just the tonic we needed.

Finally it was decision time. The meeting took about two hours. Certainly we were all in a very positive frame of mind after the Emerging Springboks result and our performance in the match. The front row took a bit of talking through. The hookers had sorted themselves out after a great old tussle during the tour. Keith Wood came through very well against Natal while Barry Williams had shown up strongly against Gauteng. Mark Regan asked what he had to do to make the grade and we told him not that much. We did not want him to change the broad approach of his game, just to try and work on his reading of it: when he should be in the tight, when he could afford to be on the fringes, and so on.

Mark Regan and Neil Back were both in contention for a place in the Test side.

Keith Wood gave us that bit more dynamism around the field. Barry, to be fair, had done well in this area too. Keith's weakness had been his throwing in, but we changed his technique on tour and it improved accordingly. Andy Keast had done some video study and, along with Jim Telfer, worked out that Woody needed to stop the backward rocking motion before he let go of the ball. The change definitely made him more accurate.

Alongside Keith would be Tom Smith and Paul Wallace, surprise choices in some people's eyes but not in ours. Tom had come through famously on the tour. He did terrifically against Gauteng and repeated the trick against Natal. We pulled him off in that game just to give him a rest. Paul had also made the best use of his opportunity. Like Tom he is not the biggest prop in the world but we were not worried in the slightest about that. We did not want to take the Springboks on at their own game. We did not want to give them the satisfaction of getting involved in a slug-fest. We wanted to challenge them to deal with the unfamiliar, to cope with props who got in underneath them and at an angle. They just love the sheer macho world of scrummaging, coming at you hard and aggressively and taking you on. We were going to do it differently and Tom and Paul were the guys who were going to help us do that.

The choice of lock to partner Martin Johnson was a very tight call. Simon Shaw had done well during the tour but we felt that Jeremy Davidson could offer us that little bit more. Right from his very first game Jeremy had shown us that he was a terrific line-out player. He was that bit lighter than Simon so was getting up to prodigious heights. He had been incredibly enthusiastic throughout the whole tour. Our chief concern was to try and prevent him damaging our own players. He charged around during training, stood on Paul Wallace's knee, smashed Neil Back in the eye and caused many bumps to others. He developed tremendously during the tour. We had originally wanted Jeremy to play against Natal but he had a slight hamstring problem so we called in Simon who had a big game as a result, knowing, I imagine, what was at stake. It was terribly close between the two of them.

The back row was another competitive area. Rob Wainwright had shown what he could do in the right environment. He scored a hat-trick against Mpumalanga and was influential against Gauteng too. But Lawrence had been an outstanding figure on the tour, mature beyond his years. His input and attitude were first-rate.

Tim Rodber was another who could offer so much for the Lions in the back row.

We then had a difficult choice between Eric Miller and Tim Rodber. Whoever we picked there had a bearing on who we put in at open side. If we chose Eric then it was to the cost of Neil Back. We would be too light in the backrow with the pair of them. As it turned out, this is exactly what happened because we went with Eric as the original choice. He had shown great dynamic form and we felt that opposite Teichmann he would get there quickly and snap up an inside ball, or whatever. Eric had done superbly against Natal, carrying the ball with real threat and getting in behind defences. That said, Tim Rodber offered an enormous amount too, as was proven when Eric had to drop out with 'flu.

People think that selection is a precise science but it is not. Of course we weigh up the strengths and weaknesses very, very carefully, both of our own squad and of the opposition, which means that there is a lot of method underpinning our thoughts. But, quite simply, when there is so little to choose between certain players you could happily go with either of them. That was true of about five or six positions in this team. Tim Rodber proved it so. He was so outstanding in the first Test that there was no way we could leave him out for the second.

As for Neil Back, there is no superlative you would not use in praise of his performances. He had been outstanding in every game and in every phase of those games. Some fault his tackling but all I can say is that they are not looking closely enough. Against Gauteng he was magnificent. He would not have let us down at all. Richard Hill is an unsung open side, doing an awful lot of important work in among the pile of bodies. He is always there in support and

a very solid defender of the gain line.

The forward pack as a whole had a balance about it. We also wanted to move the Springboks around, to take them away from their point of strength, which is why we needed mobility too.

At scrum half Matt Dawson had stepped into Rob Howley's shoes very well. He was managing games well, organising the runners and choosing his options. The deciding factor between him and Austin was that Matt's kicking game was more consistent. In a Test match kicking is often the key to getting you in the right part of the field to exploit all your other options. Austin was enjoying the fluid style, had been influential against Gauteng and defensively was doing things he had not done before in that he was hitting on the gain line rather than drifting out for the cover tackle.

Gregor Townsend was always in the frame for first-choice fly half but I have to say that if Mike Catt had been on the tour from the beginning it might have been very interesting. Mike made an immediate impact and clearly enjoyed the freedom he was given and the style we were promoting.

In the midfield it was important to get a balance. All the centres had gone so well. Take Will Greenwood, for example, who came as our only uncapped player. He enhanced his reputation every time he took the field. He was on the top of his form and would not have been out of place in any Test team. It was a great shame he got hurt against the Free State. I would have loved to see what England might have done with him if he had gone down to Australia with them. As it was, his concussion ruled him out for two months. Allan Bateman, as I have said, was held back by his hamstring problem. Alan Tait we accommodated on the wing. As with the back row we would have been happy with any combination. Scott Gibbs was a great foil to the people around him – Gregor inside and Jerry outside. He is so strong, so intimidating to the opposition and so powerful in contact. I think the subtleties of his game are overlooked sometimes. He has got great hands too as well as near-perfect timing. People have the same failing of perception about Jerry Guscott too. We hear all about his silky running but how many notice the number of times Jerry piles into a ruck because he is the nearest man. He does it all the time.

The two wing positions went to Ieuan Evans and Alan Tait. Ieuan has tremendous experience to fall back on. He very rarely gets caught out of position which means he can handle every size and shape of wing opposite him. He was also as sharp as he had ever been in attack. John Bentley had become the cult figure of the tour. He certainly pressed his case for inclusion with some spectacular running. He needed to work more, we felt, on his following of kicks and positioning in defence. Tony Underwood was playing as well as I have seen him play of late. He was seeing the field well and coming in at pace and at good angles. His defence too against Gauteng was superb. He saved a certain try in that game when they cross-kicked to their winger. We went for Alan Tait for his defence, and for his ability to come off his line.

We wanted Neil Jenkins for all the reasons we have mentioned. Neil's general reading of a game is good too, so that even if his experience of the position was not enormous he was very quick to pick up the run of play.

These were the men we had pledged ourselves to. It could easily have been different,

as everyone in the party knew. That is why they all kept on playing, as we later saw in the magnificent win against the Free State in Bloemfontein. There was not one head which dropped in the party as a result of the selection. We were all in this together.

I had known from as far back as August 1996 how I wanted us to play and how I felt we could beat the Springboks. There was no way we were going to confront them head-on. That was exactly what they wanted us to do. The All Blacks had not beaten them that way. Nor would we. We had a team that was going to deflect their most powerful assets away from success. We knew that we had to have a pack capable of actually holding their sheer volume of strength. We were going to do this by refusing to scrummage high with them because that way you gave all the advantage to them. We set out to isolate their front five, which was a powerful unit. What we also needed was strong fringe defence, packed with players who would not only put their bodies on the line but who would be able to make quick decisions about their own positioning and role in that defence.

I felt we had picked a clever team above all else, a team which would be pliable and adaptable, one which would have ideas about how it all might go but would be able to react to the circumstances all round them. We had covered an awful lot of ground on the tour on our own game. It was to our advantage that we had been together for six weeks, not just in camp but actually playing together. We had evolved a style of play and also a spirit of play, both in attack and defence.

A touring team has to create its own hallmark, traits which give it a tangible sense of identity. Ours was the nature of our attack, in which no one shirked his duty to support and also the collective defence with everyone refusing to budge one inch and hitting the right channel at every turn to protect the line. If you keep emphasising these elements then in times of acute pressure, periods of play which occur in every single Test match, then you can reach out and remember them, find some comfort in

at No.8 and Honiball at fly half. We saw how they operated in their last six Test matches and although I was worried by the change in coach I still reckoned that this axis would be crucial. I felt I knew what the old coach, André Markgraaff, had to offer. He had brought them on well but playing to a definite style. With Carel du Plessis I was less sure what they might

Carel du Plessis and Gary Teichmann prepare the Sprinboks for their first encounter with the Lions.

knowing what everyone else was thinking and feeling. Our defence was like that. It made people gasp at times. I am certain that this is what brought us through in the end.

So much for our game. We had also given the Springbok game a thorough review. Andy Keast had done his homework well. We had focused on the Natal link, in particular between Teichmann

come up with. He was younger, ambitious and full of ideas. Carel was a great player which meant that he would have the respect of his own players even though he had no experience of coaching. I was concerned that this level of esteem might inspire the Springboks, take them out of their predictable ways. As it turned out, it proved more difficult to move the South

African out of his old mindset. It is not easily done. Carel wanted to liberate them, to open them up, but when it came to the crunch they reverted to old habits of playing up through the forwards and round the half-backs – the way of Markgraaff and many before him.

The Honiball factor was crucial. He is very physical and very strong. They try to bring two or three players in off him, Teichmann being one of them. So we had to put players into the space they intended to use to nullify the threat before it got a chance even to come into play. We would never normally defend like this. British sides tend to stand back in the line and wait. But we were going to be offensive in our defence, go up fast into that space in and around Honiball. We would put three defenders in there every time. It meant that Gregor Townsend had to be a front-line defender with either the back row or Matt Dawson filling the spaces either side to cut out the runners, be it Teichmann, Venter or even du Randt. Every time Honiball looked for one of them, all he saw

was one of our red shirts. The result was that they never got players free and Honiball had to drop deeper and deeper to get any room. The South African press wondered why they had reverted to this strategy without realising that it was not a strategy at all. It was a reaction to our deliberate pressure. The greatest compliment to its success was that Honiball was dropped after the second Test.

That was the big focus of our defensive game plan. We also thought that they would defend on the fringes of the forwards rather than over the top, so we decided to go through that route. They tend to fan off, which is why we wanted to go straight and draw in that defence which would free up our potent area of attack in midfield. Too many sides allowed them to build up a head of steam in the forwards. Their dominance in games was often a result of missed tackles or bad tackles. We were not going to let that happen. That is all they were really offering in a lot of the matches, rather than creating – putting the man or the ball through into space and moving quickly.

In essence, we decided to target their supposed area of strength – their middle five – and try to render their point of strength a point of weakness. It was a key psychological ploy. If we could match them there, make them struggle to get any influence on the game, then they might lose heart elsewhere. We attacked their strong players to force them to make decisions elsewhere. Ultimately they were not able to do so. In the first Test this is exactly what happened. They began to flap the ball around frantically in the last 20–25 minutes. This is when we became much stronger, scored our two tries and might have had a couple more.

Gregor Townsend and Lawrence Dallaglio implement the Lions' defensive strategy.

Those were our ideas, all we had to do was put them into practice. We had a good day out at Stellenbosch. The only niggle was the concern about Eric Miller, who had been left behind in bed with a high temperature. It was desperately unlucky for him. James Robson isolated him so that the bug would not spread, and gave him twenty-four hours. By Thursday morning Eric's temperature was still up but he felt a bit better in himself. As ever, we took James's advice which was that Eric would probably be great for about half an hour and then he would blow up completely. Eric was not himself convinced that this would be the case until he got out of bed on Friday morning and went for a run. He came back to the hotel absolutely shattered. He came up and admitted as much to me. It was good for him to find out for himself.

There were another couple of minor problems to sort out on Wednesday evening. Rian Oberholzer, the chief executive of the South African Rugby Football Union, had asked for a meeting with our management to discuss a couple of issues. One was the playing of the South African national anthem. It had been reported in the papers that week that the Lions, who had no anthem themselves, were insisting on abiding with tradition and not allowing the opposition to play theirs. It was complete and utter nonsense. Both Australia and New Zealand played their anthems in 1989 and 1993. It did not worry me in the slightest if the Springboks did the same.

The second point of discussion was less easy to resolve. Rian had received a letter from the International Board, who had a conference in Cape Town that same week, saying that the vests with shoulder harnesses were not to be worn in any matches. Once again the politicians were interfering unnecessarily. The southern hemisphere had worn the pads for a couple of years. Last year the IB had asked Australia why they were still wearing them. A few months before our tour the Australians were fined. Then one of them saw us wearing them in South Africa, a country where their use is widespread, and where we had had no objections at all. The problem is that the Australians associate the IB with the British and wanted their bit of retaliation. We had even had problems the day before at Wellington where we played the Emerging Boks. Both coaches, myself and Nick Mallett, were quite happy with the way things were and we had agreed to take the pressure off the referee by saying that we would sanction their use. An hour before kick-off their refereeing co-ordinator, Steve Strydom, came in to say that on no account were we to play with the vests. It's all so daft and inconsistent. You can wear the padding itself if you just strap it to your body but not if it's actually manufactured into a vest. I ask you. On top of that the IB were intending to legalise it anyway. There are not too many in our party who wear them anyway – Keith Wood, who has had shoulder problems, Tim Rodber, Neil Back The whole issue was a farce, the sort of thing which should not happen in the professional era where standardised regulations and practices should apply. Anyway, we all agreed to bite the bullet.

On Thursday morning we had a session at the Village's Club which again was quite intense. At lunchtime we announced the side to the press. Fran had originally considered delaying the announcement until maybe as late as the morning of the match itself. I argued against it. We had to practise as a team and there would be so much hounding of the players by the media – and understandably so – that in the end you might upset the players themselves, the very players you were trying to protect at all costs. I felt that we were in danger of creating a situation we were not in control of, and all for a marginal advantage. Fran listened to the argument and as ever on this trip was not afraid to change. We had the press day and that was that. The media relations were good on the trip with both sides respecting the needs of the other. It was a mature relationship, I am glad to say. It is always easier, of course, when you are winning.

That was it now for the players. They had fifty-two hours between the last training session and the match itself. I sensed that one or two of

The arrival of 6,000 fans did so much to inspire the Lions in the first Test at Newlands.

them were a bit worried that they might be fatigued after all the heavy work they had done. I was not concerned myself. They were in good shape. However, if they needed a mental pick-me-up then I was happy to give it to them.

In the afternoon I went to the airport to pick up my wife, Judy, and daughter, Heather, who had flown in. The whole atmosphere in town changed that afternoon. There was planeload after planeload landing with British and Irish supporters on them. It was a great feeling to know that they had all come 6,000 miles just to roar you on. The blood was certainly beginning to pump a bit faster as we drove back into town to the Cape Sun Hotel, where I left the family and headed back to the team base just by Newlands Stadium.

Although the players had been given the Friday off I was aware that there is a danger in giving them too much time on their own to brood. So, in mid-afternoon, we all met up to have tea and scones and a walk round the Botanical Gardens. It was no more than an hour but it took their minds off the whole thing while also, at the same time, bringing them together as a team. That Friday evening we had a team meeting which was no more than a run-through of the key themes. The little bit extra we injected was to play the team a video which I had requested from an old contact and colleague, Keith Lyons, at the Centre for Notational Analysis in Cardiff. Keith had been a great help during the season compiling videos of players which we used in selection reviews. I had asked Keith to draw up a tape which reflected people's perception of the Lions back in Britain. That was the only brief he had. Just how did we look from 6,000 miles away? What characterised the 1997 Lions?

Keith came up with a twelve-minute video which he had set to music. It was great stuff. When I first saw it, it had the hairs on the back of my neck standing up. The first six minutes of it were all of the Lions without the ball, which was entirely Keith's reading of it. The music was loud and evocative, so too was the play. It was great to see all the highlights, all the big tackling stitched together. The last half was the Lions cutting loose, streaming on to the ball at pace and in depth. Another good thing was that the clips involved all thirty-five players. I am not sure if Keith did that deliberately. When the players came into the room on Friday evening I said nothing but just switched the tape on and let it run. It had the desired effect. This was what we were about – a unified party intent on playing good, hard rugby.

We were kicking-off at 5.15, so we had to manage the hours of the day quite carefully. Jim and I took a session with the non-Test team that morning. They needed it in the build-up for their next game and it was right and proper that they should feel involved. When we got back to the hotel about 11.30, I decided to nip over the road to the girls' school opposite to ask the guard at the gates there if we could just have a run-out in one corner of the fields for fifteen to twenty minutes that lunchtime. I knew that there were corporate hospitality marquees there, but the guard was sure no one would object. Quite the opposite, in fact. I should think it added a few bob to the bill to be able to see the Lions warm up for a Test match.

I had kept a close eye on the weather reports because there was a big front on its way in from the Atlantic. It was cloudier than it had been first thing, but it still looked as if the bad weather would hit after the match had finished,

which, I am glad to say, is exactly what happened. You can do no more than taper your game if it rains. Jim and I had also had a chat that morning with the referee, Colin Hawke, just to outline our concerns about various phases of play, such as the tackle and the ball-in-contact situations. We were also keen to hear his views on the scrum engagement. It was too late to go back and really brief the players on everything, and he would be having a word himself before kick-off. In the long run, though, you might be able to get referees to see your point of view.

As the match approached, Martin Johnson came more and more into his own. Martin was doing exactly what we wanted him to do. He was not making any attempt to be anybody but Martin Johnson. He does not speak unless something is worth saying, does not bother too much with any gimmicks or psychological ploys to get the boys going. He is not officious or over the top. He allows other people their say and leans heavily on the senior players. It is a different style from many captains but it does not matter one little bit. It is effective.

The drive from the hotel to the ground was no more than two minutes. In fact, given the traffic, it would have been quicker to walk. But the sight of all the crowds and colourful stalls really brought it home to the players what a Test match meant to the outside world. Stan Bagshaw, our logistics man, and the medical staff always got to the ground an hour earlier than the team in order to lay everything out. So when they walked in, the first thing they saw was their jersey hanging up. This is a striking moment for any player.

And suddenly it was kick-off time. All that planning, all those hours spent poring over a video machine, all that effort and energy, were now distilled into the first blast of the referee's whistle. And what happened? We did everything we said we would not do in those first fifteen minutes. We went high in the first scrum and they came piling through. We gave them such an easy ride in that opening spell. We did not clear our lines, they kicked a goal, they kicked back again and we were on the back foot. But already it was clear that we were defending well. They expected us to cave in but we did not. They got that early penalty but we got one back in the sixth minute through Neil Jenkins. It was a good drive up the middle which created that position. We went at them low and hard which

showed that we could play a bit too. Lubbe missed a chance eight minutes later. Although we had not seen much of the ball, it actually helped us because the confidence we got from defending stayed with us through the entire game. I think our solidity there also sapped their resolve a little too.

We were not giving too many penalties away either. One that we did enabled them to kick for position in the corner from where du Randt barrelled his way over from the line out. We got our body positions all wrong, a mistake which we rectified for the second Test when they tried to do the same.

Gary Teichmann points the way, but this time Russell Bennett's try was disallowed.

Ruben Kruger looks on in disbelief as Matt Dawson outsmarts the cover defence to score the try that gave the Lions the lift they needed for the final minutes of the first Test. (Below) Alan Tait touches down to seal victory for the Lions.

Obviously they got heart from the score but we were not fazed by that. Neil knocked his penalty goals over and then it was half-time and we were in front, 9–8. We talked at half-time primarily about keeping ball. We had to be patient because they were not threatening us and we had showed that we could create. We knew that they would put in a big fifteen minutes again after the interval and we just had to ride that. Unfortunately we gave a stupid try away just four minutes after the restart, Scott Gibbs, of all people, missing a tackle. Teichmann got in behind and put the

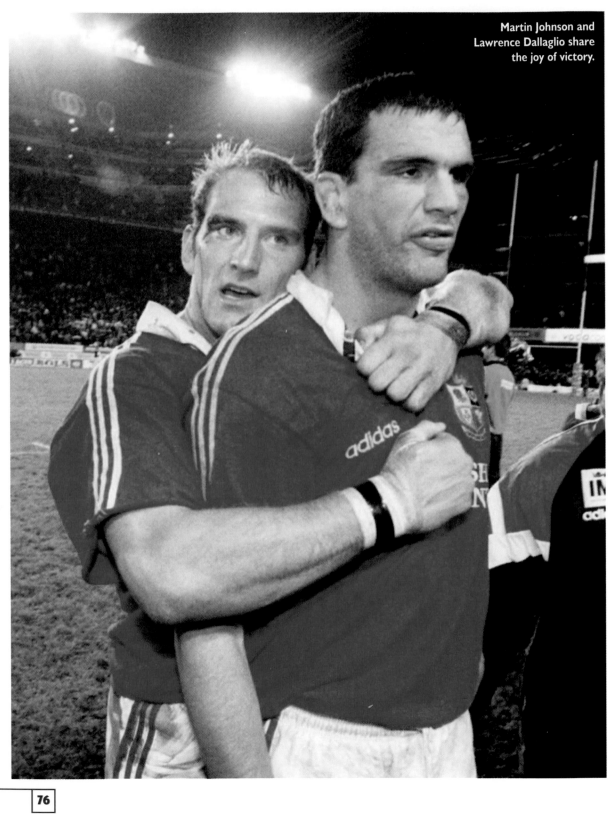

Martin Johnson and
Lawrence Dallaglio share
the joy of victory.

The Welsh connection, Ieuan Evams and Neil Jenkins, celebrate at the final whistle.

replacement, Russell Bennett, in at the corner. It highlighted what we had said all along, that if you gave them a sniff then they would score. But it was our mistake which had given them the opportunity. They still were not doing anything to cause us real problems. Honiball's penalty made it 16–12, Jenks having kicked a goal in the first minute of the second half. He put another one over in the 61st minute to make it 16–15, vindication if it were needed of having a goal-kicker in your side.

As the clock ticked down I was quite happy. We were beginning to make more and more of the plays. And then came Matt Dawson's try. It was a brilliant piece of opportunism which I think chimed with the mood of the tour. If you think something is possible then it's no good just thinking about it – go out and do it. Matt

had the confidence to call the play and the self-belief, nerve and cheek to put it into action. Ironically it was just what everyone expected van der Westhuizen to do – to break from a scrum position and be a threat. The quality of the player who took Matt's dummy was amazing. We all went up in the air on the bench. It was just the lift we needed with just seven minutes to go. We then got better and better.

We had the initiative, forcing them to play in areas in which they were not comfortable. We finished them off with a good try. Drive up the middle, quick ball, Scott Gibbs hammering to the posts and then out left where Tim Rodber had the vision to throw a long pass, Jenks passed it on, and in went Alan Tait. It was a brilliant way to finish. A long night of celebration beckoned.

What they said after the first Test

Martin Johnson: *It is something we have dreamed about but it is no good winning one Test and losing two. If we win two, we'll have something to shout about. It could have gone either way, Matt's try turned it for us.*

They really took us on at the first scrum and pushed us back a few yards, which was a bit unnerving but we had to keep going. Credit to Tom Smith, Keith Wood and Paul Wallace who kept working. When South Africa put the pressure through, they were one of the strongest scrums I have played against.

The standard of play we have produced has surprised a lot of people, maybe some of the players on this tour. We still have to get used to the physicality of the southern-hemisphere style. The forwards have picked up on that and the Rugby League guys have helped. If we win the series we can go home and say this is a starting block for us to improve our rugby, to compete with the southern-hemisphere nations.

Fran Cotton: *We picked the side honestly, based on performance, but it wasn't just the fifteen boys who did it but all thirty-five players. The support of the boys on the field was superb.*

Matt Dawson: *The initial platform was set by the forwards. Because we had to control, I could get on the outside of the defence and away. It was the initial ten yards that made it [his try]. The second half felt a lot quicker than the first. There was a lot of close-quarter work in the first half that the forwards found physically demanding.*

Alan Tait: *It [the victory] started six months ago, this dream, and it is still going on. This is probably the best fixture I have ever played in. The defence was awesome from the lads. I don't think we had the credit we deserved but today we earned respect.*

Carel du Plessis: *The match was one of lost opportunities. We made mistakes, gave away possession and that was costly in the end. The back-line performance was very disappointing. Sometimes possession was slow, we weren't playing off a decent platform. We must pick up the pace of our game and I'm confident the players can still do it, that they can step up as a team. The Lions had their share of the game, their defence was solid and they were prepared to take it to the man [in possession]. But I believe our team is able to do better, the right combinations are still in place and I'm confident in their ability. We have to work on the indiscipline, not giving away penalties which is free possession.*

Gary Teichmann: *The Lions' defence was well organised. We got past the first line but the cover defence was great. The more you play together the better you get. The Lions have just come together and they are a good side.*

The Lions scrummed well, they held their own. I thought at one stage we might put a bit more pressure on, and were starting to dominate but they came back well. We spent a lot of time in their half but we weren't getting the points. We had opportunities and didn't take them, and that's a major concern. The Lions were lying very flat and the kick was on but maybe at times we should have kept it in hand. The pressure will build up on us but we have been through that experience. The series is still open, the guys are still very positive. There might be concern if we had lost really badly but we are still in the game.

convert your business potential

KPMG
means business

IT'S TIME YOU MADE THE CONVERSION.

When it comes to 4x4's, nothing quite matches a Land Rover.

Whether you're looking for the uncompromising strength and endurance of Defender, the versatility and comfort of Discovery, or the sheer luxury of the Range Rover, no other family of vehicles provides you with so many options, regardless of the season or conditions.

If you're currently disenchanted with the limitations of your ordinary vehicle, or maybe just curious as to what Land Rover can do for you, Freephone 100, ask for Land Rover and we'll be happy to provide you with more information.

Because it really is time you took a shot at something different.

 **THE BEST 4x4xFAR**

For details of your nearest Land Rover dealer call Freephone 100 Land Rover or write to - Land Rover, Freepost TK 494, Twickenham TW2 5UN. Fax to: 0181 894 3099

5. THE SECOND TEST

These things always take a long time to sink in. In the stadium there is so much going on, and still so much to do by way of formal receptions that you rarely get a chance to step back and take on board just what has happened. My immediate feeling was simply one of relief, that all the good rugby we had played up to the Test had been vindicated by a win. Any tour has to be judged by the criterion of how you fare in the Tests. It would have been so sad if, having put together some great rugby, we had lost and been seen as complete failures. But we had not.

There was the inevitable debate in the South African media as to whether we had been good or the Boks bad. They all leaned towards the latter. There was much made too about what might have been if the pass to Bennett, the replacement winger, towards the end of the match had not been called forward. Well, it was forward, of that there is no doubt. However, even if it had not been spotted and the try scored to make it 21–15 (at least) to South Africa, I still feel we might have won it. One of the qualities of this team was its ability to claw things back. They did not panic and they were patient. Only the great sides have been able to do that.

You think how many times you have seen an All Black side not really in control and apparently struggling and then, wham, suddenly they have scored two tries in the last fifteen minutes and the game's gone. It happened to England when they played the New Zealand Barbarians. We were doing to South Africa what they and the Kiwis have done to many teams down the years – absorb pressure

and then strike. That is what I took from the Newlands Test. We kept playing rugby under the cosh. You do not get the opportunity to score two tries if you are not scrummaging well and working the field. Our scrum, which is a small unit, did superbly.

We had not only put on a show for our supporters in the crowd, we had also done it in front of nearly the entire International Board who had been in Cape Town all week for a conference. It was good to see them at the reception afterwards and know that none of them could be disparaging again about northern-hemisphere rugby. That was the beauty of it all. We had put ourselves back on the map.

Saturday evening actually turned out to be quiet. Everyone was so drained by the experience that there was little desire to go out and paint the town red. We all went out for a meal together near Newlands at the Cantina Tequila but were back in the hotel at midnight where, would you believe, I ended up in the team room watching a video of the match and talking rugby with a few of the players, Tim Rodber, Rob Wainwright, Barry Williams and Keith Wood. You see, we just could not get enough of it.

It was on the way to that evening's dinner that Martin Johnson had come up to me on the coach and said that the Test team wanted to turn out at training the next day and help hold the tackle bags for the others. It was a magnificent gesture and one which summed up the squad ethos. The weather was not that great but the boys were there.

We had our usual coaches' meeting on Sunday evening, having flown into Durban from Cape Town that afternoon. We looked at ways we might improve. Even though the defence had been magnificent, we thought we could still add a notch or two. Our defensive system had made their very good players look ordinary. Our players were so disciplined, getting to the right place at the right time to fill the necessary channel. Honiball, in particular, found it more and more difficult to move. The more anxious he became, the more our players began to feed off each other. I do not think the South Africans ever really worked out what we were doing in that area of the field. All they could think of doing was to drop Honiball after the second Test.

Their frustration also came from our refusal to panic, to get edgy, lose shape and self-control. We gave away only three penalties in the second half at Newlands (and only one the following week in Durban) which was testimony to our commitment in practice and our composure out on the field. We had worked on defence at nearly every training session, anything from five minutes to fifty minutes. All the time I kept hammering home the importance of going six inches back from the offside line so as not to give them the merest sniff. It all paid off. The Rugby League boys were at home here. Communication is big with them. You could tell when it was working well in training because it was very, very noisy.

We thought at that Sunday meeting that we could make better use of the blind side and that we could move them around more. We also expected them to place more emphasis in the second Test on strategic kicking, which in fact they did.

It was to be a demanding week. We had to regroup for the backlash to come at King's Park but also take time out to go to Bloemfontein for possibly the hardest provincial fixture of all against the Free State, another Super 12 side. We had decided back in the UK that only the match party of twenty-one players would travel for the Tuesday game, leaving the bulk of the Test party behind. I know it sounds divisive, particularly when we were so big on maintaining squad harmony. But the players had all agreed with us back in London that it was the best use of time and resources. No one objected at all.

We were to fly up on Tuesday morning, arriving in mid-afternoon for the evening kick-off. It was a very tight schedule. I had intended to go but had fallen ill on Monday evening with some sort of 'flu bug. Even so, I was keen to make the trip. It was only forty-five minutes before we were due to take off that James Robson strongly advised that I stay at the hotel. As much as anything James was worried that in the close confines of a plane the bug would spread more easily.

I stayed in Durban and watched in awe at what I thought was our most complete performance of the tour. The quality of rugby and the levels of continuity were first-rate. Make no mistake either, this was a very good side against us, all fired up and determined to lower our colours. To win 52–30 and to sustain our style and shape the way we did was fantastic. It gave the boys watching back in Durban an enormous lift. I began to feel a lot better too.

We had asked Ollie Redman to be captain for the day. His reaction when I broke the news to him was wonderful. He looked at me as if he could not believe what he was hearing. I knew that he would do the job properly and cope with

Tony Underwood rounds the cover defence
on his way to a try against Free State.

turn was to make the adversity a positive, to focus as soon as they left Durban that morning and ignore the flight, the hanging around in a crowded hotel and all the little niggles.

The one major blot on a fantastic evening was the injury to Will Greenwood. Will was, as usual on the tour, in sublime form, finding space where others struggled to. Then, in the 39th minute, he was thrown heavily to the ground in a tackle. Even from a distance I knew it was a bad fall, his head banging on to the hard ground. In my worst nightmares I could not have imagined just how horrific it actually was.

James Robson was on the pitch in an instant. Will was out cold and was to remain so for six minutes. Even though someone is unconscious, there is usually some reaction to light on the pupils. With Will there was none. You only have five minutes to get some before you pronounce the person brain-dead. That was what James feared with Will. Four minutes had passed and

the difficult circumstances surrounding the match. Ollie is a top tourist, aware that the hassles can easily distract. What he managed in

Mark Davies calls for a stretcher as James Robson attends to the unconscious Will Greenwood.

still nothing. James rushed him off the pitch and had the knife in the tunnel ready to do an emergency opening of the airways. The only thing which kept Will going was the fact that his gumshield had prevented his teeth from clamping together and a minute amount of air was getting through.

James kept trying to force the mouth open, saying all the time, 'Come on, Will, get your mouth open. Let's get the gumshield out.' It was music from heaven when he suddenly heard Will parrot those exact words back to him even though he was still unconscious. It was as close as that, a terrible, terrible scenario to contemplate.

I was not aware of any of this. I actually took a phone call from Will in the hospital later that evening. He was anxious to know the final score. The rest of the squad were already on the charter back to Durban. The people at the hospital in Bloemfontein were terrific. Will had had a full brain scan within thirty minutes of the incident. It revealed no lasting problems. He had actually broken the shoulder joint in the process but that was the least of the worries. James recommended that Will take two months off from any sort of contact sport.

Once again we all had reason to be grateful to James Robson. Will did a TV interview before the second Test and said that he would like to send a message to James's wife and daughter back in the UK to thank them for letting James come on tour because he had saved his life. Catherine, James's wife, said she spent the entire match in tears after hearing that.

I had worked with James a lot when I was coaching Scotland. He is not only a qualified doctor, he is also a qualified physiotherapist which means he understands so much of what it takes to get a player back on the field. Medical qualifications apart, he is also a great human being. No one has a bad word for him. He has a great rapport with the players which is invaluable. I thought he had worked miracles when he got Gavin Hastings on the field for me in the second Test in New Zealand in 1993. After Bloemfontein I now know the true meaning of working miracles. Will, we were all truly thankful to say, was with us in the team room by one o'clock the next day.

We had two sessions that Wednesday, both of them sharp and intense. For the unscheduled evening training, Andy Keast had found us a ground out along the south Durban coast, where Harlequins play. The lights were good, there was a crowd of Brits around and once again you could feel that nervous, excited edge about everything and everyone. We knew the side we wanted even though we were not going to announce it until Thursday. The only doubt surrounded Ieuan Evans who had a lingering groin problem. We were not quite sure how long to give him to prove his fitness but, in the end, Ieuan decided it for us. He came in off his right foot in training and collapsed like a sack of potatoes. The groin was no longer just a pull. It was now a tear and, sadly, Ieuan was on his way home. I had been with him all the way through so it was upsetting to see it all end in anti-climax. Ieuan's a marvellous competitor and a great bloke to boot.

So John Bentley it was, the man who was awake at 5 a.m. and peering down the hotel corridor to wait for Sam Peters to post the letters under the doors. That was our only change in the starting line-up. The main focus of our discussions concerned the bench. We wanted to have more flexibility there so that we could make tactical switches rather than just replace someone through injury. We went for four forwards and two backs rather than the normal three and three split. We wanted to be able to change the focus of our game, which is why we wanted Eric Miller and Neil Back on the bench. If push came to shove, then Neil could play out in the backs. The two backs were Mike Catt and Austin Healey, both of whom were very versatile. As it was, Austin came on to play on the wing.

Changing a winning team is always a difficult call. You have to consider the momentum of the team dynamics, and that those in form deserve the opportunity to play. However you then have to gauge how the breaking up of a successful unit will affect those still left in the side. We left well alone, although, as I have often said, there were four or five players who would not be out of place at all in a Lions Test team.

The Springboks had made changes behind the pack with Percival Montgomery and Pieter Rossouw getting first caps in the centre and on the wing. The Northern Transvaal centre, Danie van Schalkwyk, was also brought in. We did not spend an undue amount of time worrying about them. We showed the players a video excerpt on Wednesday evening but only for them to familiarise themselves. Our main concern was to brief them about the intensity of the Springbok riposte that Saturday. We talked again and again about what the surge would be like, how they would come at them like dervishes and then come again. They certainly did not disappoint us on that front.

There was actually a lot of illegal play in what they did, often taking out the players beyond the ball and blocking the way so that their runners could get in. Matt Dawson was blatantly blocked at one point by Venter clearing a path

Wrapped! An injury to Ieuan Evans would mean a Lions Test debut for John Bentley in the second Test.

through. There were also a couple of unsavoury incidents with van Heerden kicking Jerry Guscott on the floor and then punching Tom Rodber late in the game. In a Test match you expect massive collisions. It was not pretty but I had no intention of citing. I was furious with Northern Transvaal for citing Scott Gibbs and I

The England back row of Lawrence Dallaglio, Tim Rodber and Richard Hill were magnificent in the first Test.

The Irish contingent – Keith Wood, Jeremy Davidson, Paul Wallace and Eric Miller stroll along the Durban beach.

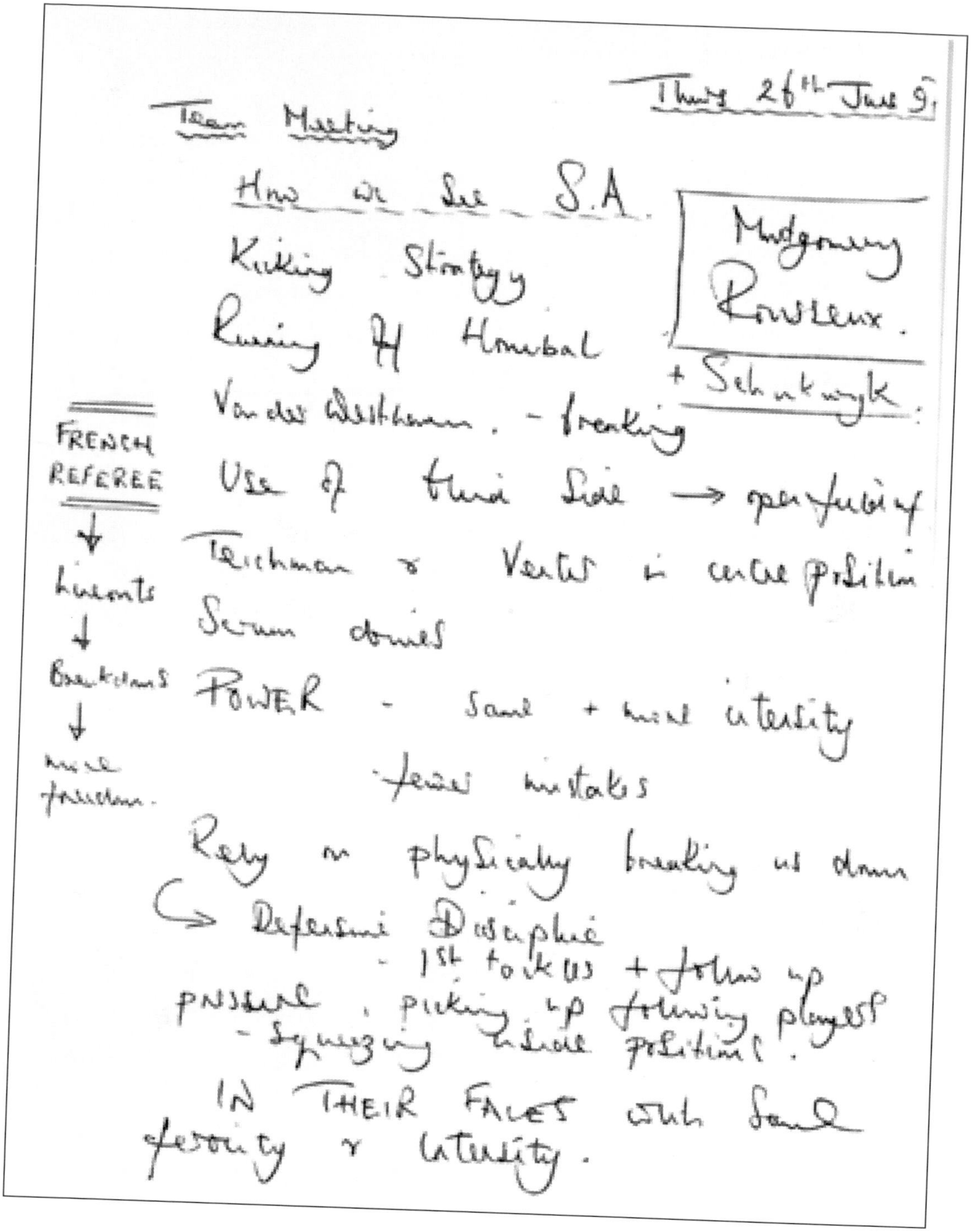

Thurs 26th June 9?

Team Meeting

How we See S.A.

Kicking Strategy

Running of Hourbal

Van der Westhum. – Breaking

FRENCH
REFEREE
↓
Lumonts
↓
Breakdowns
↓
more
frustran.

Mudgomery
Roulenx.
+ Schutwyk.

Use of third Side → open fuebing

Teichman & Venter in centre position

Scrum domies

POWER – Same + more intensity

fewer mistakes

Rely on physically breaking us down
↳ Defensive Discipline
– 1st to ick us + follow up
pressure. picking up following players
– Squeezing inside positions.
IN THEIR FACES with Same
ferocity & intensity.

A page from Ian McGeechan's notes for the second Test.

did not want to be as petty as they had been. There is a clear line between the Bosmans of this world and the fevered energy of the Springboks in Durban.

Durban was being flooded with British supporters, many of whom were in our hotel. The noise and atmosphere on the day itself was unbelievable so we could hardly complain if our hotel had been a bit loud and crowded in the build-up. We had a team night out at the Langoustine seafood restaurant on the Thursday evening to keep faith with our Lions Laws which said we should have at least one outing a week all together.

The following day I took the squad to the Bird Gardens in order to get them to relax a little. It was only for about an hour and a quarter but the people there laid on a special show with owls, vultures and eagles, finishing off with a performance by the flamingos on the lake. It may sound the exact opposite of what you imagine rugby players might be doing on the eve of a Test but, as we have said before, you want players to unwind not get steamed up. We had our final meetings. We knew the general line – right person, right pass, right place, right time, all the time. It was a simple creed. If we played to it and were patient we were in the ball game. But we had to weather the storm.

On the way to the ground the players were very quiet. It was no more than a fifteen-minute drive and I was just a touch anxious that they were not getting too much inside themselves. It could make them tighten up and not play. They knew that the Boks would come at them. It is what they always did – route one. So much of

Neil Jenkins's boot would prove the difference between the two sides.

their strategy is based on the belief that eventually someone will miss a tackle. In the final analysis we did not miss many and that is why we won.

the death to allow the Boks an easy route back into our half. We spent more than two-thirds of that half on the back foot, which makes it extremely difficult not to give away points

Joost van der Westhuizen evades the grasp of Keith Wood to score the first try at Durban.

The game lived up to expectations. They were like wild men for the first quarter of an hour yet had nothing to show for it. We had one slender opening and Neil Jenkins banged the penalty over from 45 metres. He did the same fifteen minutes later to make it 6–0. We were actually creating a bit too but were making mistakes at

particularly against a side as good as South Africa. I thought they got a rough ride from their press. They had a lot of good players in there who would have come through if we had only let them.

Their first try by van der Westhuizen in the 35th minute came from a slight lapse by us,

André Joubert gives South Africa a 15–9 lead.

Keith Wood allowing him to step inside. If your defenders get caught one behind the other, rather than being side by side, then you are vulnerable. As happened in Cape Town there was not much between the teams. I told the players at half-time that we needed to relax, keep the ball and they would make mistakes. We had to be patient, that was all.

Unfortunately, as in the first Test, we gave away a try right after the restart. Alan Tait tried to force it a bit too much and flipped the ball behind him in defence. Unfortunately it went straight to Honiball who shipped it on to Montgomery who scored. Neil Jenkins got us three points back shortly afterwards only for Joubert to score a try in the 54th minute to take South Africa 15–9 clear. Again it was an error, this time John Bentley going too high and getting pushed off by Joubert. I still was not that concerned because we were within a score of them. The only worry was that the tries would help the Springboks to relax, that they would play with more confidence and begin to spread it wide. They did not get the chance.

The way we came back surprised even me. From somewhere the boys found the fortitude to get back down the park. The revival was not quite as obvious or striking as at Cape Town, where we got two tries, but it was decisive nonetheless. People may say we won it through penalties and a drop goal. But you do not get those opportunities unless you are in position, unless your forward play is solid and consistent. Jenks put his fourth penalty over in the 65th minute and his next, the equalising one, nine minutes later. Then came the charge to glory.

Believe it or not, there were better options than for Keith Wood to wallop the ball upfield. He had men outside him in fact. Luckily they fumbled and we got the lineout. From hereon in we were superb. It was a great take and drive, Gregor had a go and then, with the ball recycled, Jerry spotted his chance. He took position and, bang, over she went. I was up out of the seat, of course, as was Jim Telfer alongside me. We were up in the main stand so as to get a higher view and were surrounded by South African supporters. Let us just say that Jim let them know how he felt.

There were other good things in that last quarter. Neil Back had come on for Richard Hill and showed up well. Austin Healey did

Jeremy Guscott's dropped goal sails past Henry Honiball on its way through the posts to seal victory for the Lions.

Fran Cotton and John Bentley celebrate the series victory.

brilliantly, after replacing Alan Tait, to help Neil Jenkins and stop a try. Yet again we were the side who finished the better. It is a trait of the All Blacks, to play the game right to the very last second. That is what we were doing.

I could not really believe it, I suppose, when the final whistle went. The players were all there on the pitch applauding the supporters who had been magnificent. Jim and I joined them. The atmosphere was incredible. It was just good to see the players so happy, to know that they had got the reward and the recognition for all that work they had put in. There was a real sense of shared fulfilment among us all.

It was all very different to 1974. It is a close call, but I think this series win gave me more satisfaction for the simple reason that we had been written off so extensively beforehand. In 1974 British rugby was on a high in world terms. Here few people gave us a prayer, so it was nice to make them eat humble pie.

I suppose even I was one of those who doubted that we would have it all wrapped up by the end of the second Test. When the players were getting their pre-tour haircuts in London before departure, I agreed to have a close crop if we went 2–0 up. Within five minutes of the final whistle, Matt Dawson and Austin Healey were reminding me of what I had said. There was no escape. It was back to the hotel and the team room where my hair fell to the floor. It was not a pretty sight but it was well worth it

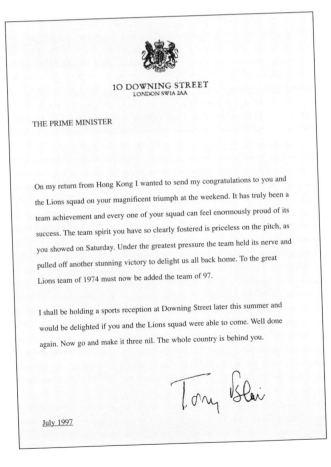

(Left) Tony Blair's fax to congratulate the squad after the second Test. (Below) Victory meant a severe haircut for the Lions' coach – by Keith Wood the barber.

10 DOWNING STREET
LONDON SW1A 2AA

THE PRIME MINISTER

On my return from Hong Kong I wanted to send my congratulations to you and the Lions squad on your magnificent triumph at the weekend. It has truly been a team achievement and every one of your squad can feel enormously proud of its success. The team spirit you have so clearly fostered is priceless on the pitch, as you showed on Saturday. Under the greatest pressure the team held its nerve and pulled off another stunning victory to delight us all back home. To the great Lions team of 1974 must now be added the team of 97.

I shall be holding a sports reception at Downing Street later this summer and would be delighted if you and the Lions squad were able to come. Well done again. Now go and make it three nil. The whole country is behind you.

Tony Blair

July 1997

'2–0 to us,' says Jeremy Guscott, as he poses for the cameras with Martin Johnson and Neil Jenkins.

What they said after the second Test

Martin Johnson: *We talked about how South Africa would come at us all week. But there is talking and there is doing. Jenks kept us in the game. It was frustrating, the mistakes we made, we didn't hold on to the ball in too many phases of play. But we found a way to win the Test series. It has been a massive squad effort, they should all be proud of themselves.*

There have been many great characters, some great leadership on this tour and everyone – and the management – can be proud. We said that if we won the series it would be the biggest achievement in our careers, and right now it's my best day in rugby.

Jeremy Guscott: *We got into a position where we were going to call a dropped goal anyway. Gregor was a bit out of it. The move went left and Matt looked up, looking for Gregor and saw me. There was panic all over his face but it was a sweet pass and I just thought, 'Drop goal'. Then I thought, 'What if I miss?' but I didn't, it sailed between the posts, three points, a Test series, thank you very much.*

Neil Jenkins: *It's a huge day. I have been on the wrong end of a few hidings from South Africa, with Wales, and to come through here today was a great achievement. The kicks cost them at the end of the day. They put a lot more kicks through on me this week and a couple of times I dropped them, but Austin covered up at the end. The back three, all the backs, have worked really hard this week.*

Fran Cotton: *I don't think anything has been better than this in my experience. The players, from day one, have had a tremendous attitude towards the tour and towards each other. That [victory] was dug out of sheer character. We hung on and in the end we had a* chance and took it. You don't always get your just rewards in life but these players have. We came here 5–2 against [on the betting] but we told people from day one we could do it. Already the feedback from home is that people have been enjoying the kind of rugby we play, which is important. But there is nothing better than winning a series to stimulate interest. It can only be good for British and Irish rugby.*

Carel du Plessis: *It was an important one for us and we missed the opportunity. That's a big disappointment. The decisions [of the referee] don't always go your way but that's something the coaching staff have to live with. We should be more disciplined and limit the number of penalties against us. The place kicking cost us a few points. We scored three tries and it wasn't good enough. We must give the Lions credit for staying in the match, for being able to come back.*

We have improved from last week and we can still do better. We have played positive rugby, we have done well, there is no crisis.

Gary Teichmann: *We have to look at the goal kicking and some opportunities we missed but I must say I was very happy with the improvement. We had a lot of disruptions and the young guys who came in did very well. It's hard to believe we lost. I feel we had the game. We gave away a couple of penalties which let them back into our half. We always have a game plan but a lot depends on how the game runs for you. We wanted to get into them at the beginning, put them on the back foot. We wanted to put the ball behind them, put pressure on Jenkins and it worked pretty well. We gave everything we had but things didn't run for us, and that happens.*

ONE NAME ALWAYS LIVES UP TO THE CHALLENGE.

Guts, individualism and supremacy. Three vital attributes you'll find in all the most successful teams.

Little coincidence, then, that they are also the foundation stones upon which the Land Rover marque is built.

Let's kick off with Defender. Designed as the ultimate workhorse, no other vehicle combines raw strength and total driveability so effectively. It is hardly surprising that it has earned a reputation as the toughest 4x4 ever built.

If it's an all-round player you're looking for, get to grips with a Discovery. With a choice of 3.9 litre V8i petrol or 2.5 litre Tdi diesel engine and up to seven seats, its supreme versatility means it tackles business or leisure outings with equal relish.

Which leaves the Range Rover. The last word in comfort, Range Rover effortlessly pushes forward into areas where other luxury vehicles fear to tread.

For more information, Freephone 100 and ask for Land Rover.

THE BEST 4x4xFAR

For details of your nearest Land Rover dealer call Freephone 100 Land Rover or write to - Land Rover, Freepost TK 494, Twickenham TW2 5UN. Fax to: 0181 894 3099

International Teamwork

Whether you're an individual
or a team player,
we'll support you all the way

6. THE THIRD TEST

We had our usual Sunday coaching meeting up on the high veldt in Vereeniging, some 50 miles from Johannesburg, where we had flown that afternoon. We looked at each other. Silence.

'Er, what now?' said someone.

I do not know how many of us thought we really would be in this position. It was mission accomplished. The series had been won 2–0 and suddenly we had a totally different sort of week in prospect. The whole ball game had changed simply because the ball game itself had been won. Did it feel good? You bet it did. And, yes, it had sunk in pretty quickly. It could not be otherwise. There had been so many British supporters in and around the team hotel in Durban wandering about with a happy dazed look on their faces that you knew something quite extraordinary had happened. They were all bubbling emotionally, on an absolute delirious high, that you could not help but be affected by it. You might have wanted to keep your feet on the ground but they just kept dragging you skywards. It was a wonderful day.

Although there was a huge amount of noise and singing from the young supporters in the bars and hotel lobbies, backing which had been crucial during the matches, it was the look on the faces of some of the older fans which made the most impression on me. Several couples came up to me and just said, 'Thank you,' before walking away. That was it. It meant so much to them. Here they were, having probably saved for a couple of years for the trip of a lifetime and it had turned out so marvellously well. You have to remember that, historically, the Lions do not win that often. There was no doubt that for them it was a Max Boyce weekend – I was there – one they would be able to recall for ever and a day.

It is the impact you have on other people's lives which makes all the hard work worthwhile. You do it all for yourself and the team, of course, because you enjoy what you are doing for its own sake. But what elevates it into something truly special is the way it is all appreciated by other people, by the effect it has on them too. I remember Jim Telfer saying something to me on the eve of our Grand Slam decider with England in 1990. We had gone for a walk and a cup of tea on the Friday afternoon.

'You know,' said Jim, 'If we win tomorrow these young men will never be the same again. You won't be the same again. That's how much one event can change things. You and they will have got to a place few people ever reach.'

I recalled those words shortly after waking on that Sunday morning in Durban. It was different and it was special and I was somewhere else. You could see it in the players' faces, too. This whole group would never be the same again. They had reached very privileged territory. The whole experience would be with them for the rest of their lives. It would never go away, merely grow and glow at different times.

Mind you, it was hard to read the faces of one or two of them for they were looking very bleary. And why not? This was the most dedicated bunch I had ever worked with. We had had a big night out after the Natal game but had been more or less tucked up by midnight after the first Test. This was only the second night that they had let their hair down, three nights in all if you count the following weekend. It would never have been tolerated in my day. After the Durban Test I had had a meal and bottle of red wine with Jim Telfer and Judy, my wife. I am not one for too much drinking. A lot of the players headed back to King's Park in the early hours to join the barbecues still going on. It was a great party by all accounts. It had been a great day there, too. If anyone tells you that professional rugby is all wrong, then refer them back to Durban. The whole atmosphere was first-rate. Barbecues before, dramatic rugby, and then parties afterwards until three in the morning all around the stadium. Where's the wrong in all that? I heard that Keith Wood had gone off for an early morning swim in the Indian Ocean. He thought better of it and laid his head on the sands for a quiet nap, laying his four-pack of beers alongside. When he woke it was dawn and the beers had gone. It was the only thing the South Africans got away with all weekend.

We headed north, to Van der Byl Park. It was billed as a resort leisure complex, away from the hustle and distractions of Jo'burg. I imagine that it was booked with a view to us hardening our focus in the build-up to a series that would be decided in Ellis Park. Let us just say that it was ideal for a spot of Spartan preparation. As John Bentley said: 'I would have hated to see where they'd have sent us if we'd lost.' I think it was the sulphur fumes belching out from the nearby chemical plants which did not quite tickle Bentos's fancy.

It was the one flaw in all our arrangements. That said, the hotel staff were very obliging and the facilities at the stadium nearby were in good order too. After the euphoria of Sunday it was important to lay down a few markers for the week on the Monday morning. Fran spoke and congratulated everyone. I then told them how crucial it was that we all stuck together for eight more days. And the real onus on the success of this last week lay with the non-Test players. If the tour was to end on a high, they had to stay as part of the whole thing, no matter what might happen in the final Test itself. It would be a desperate shame to put even a minor blight on the experience.

I am not sure I even needed to spell it out for them. They were such a good bunch of blokes, mature, honest and committed, that they would have worked it out for themselves. Even those who hurt inside at missing out on Test places – Graham Rowntree, Simon Shaw, Barry Williams and many others – were all supportive and uncomplaining through that entire week, holding bags at training, giving advice and encouragement. I think these will be the memories which will stay with me – of a great group of individuals helping each other out every minute of every day.

The week needed careful management. James Robson advised that many of the players were on their last legs and needed at least three days' recovery. We gave it to them. It was a question of striking the balance between mental and physical recovery, between letting the bodies recuperate and sharpening the mind once again for a torrid examination in the Test match. The Test team did not train until Wednesday. They all still, however, insisted on travelling to Welkom, a couple of hours' drive away, for the final midweek match against Northern Free Sate.

We were also hit in that last week by an outbreak of 'flu. At one point there were 17 players sidelined with a gastric bug. We were in the same hotel in Johannesburg as the All Blacks had been prior to the World Cup Final in 1995. They had been stricken by food poisoning the night before the game, which lead to lurid conspiracy tales of a mysterious waitress named Susie doctoring their food. This illness was altogether more straightforward. It was a virus pure and simple. Most of the boys recovered within twenty-four hours. Only Tim Rodber failed to make it and was replaced on the morning of the third Test by Rob Wainwright.

For all the ailments the last week was the best I have ever been involved in. In 1989, and again in 1993, the series was still to be decided. In '93 the camp had divided. In Australia, four years before that, the party was strong also. It was just that the entire squad here were on the ball right to the final whistle. For example, Graham Rowntree played on the Tuesday against Northern Free State and then had to take a full part in the scrummaging session the

Tony Underwood leaves Northern Free State defender, Willie Nagel, in his wake, on his way to one of his hat-trick of tries.

next day because Tom Smith had gone down ill. Graham, who was obviously sorely disappointed at missing out, never once murmured a complaint. So too Allan Bateman, a player I had the highest regard for. It was obvious from our Wednesday practice that we had again left him out of the starting line-up even though he was eventually to be on the bench. He dutifully manned the tackle bags again and urged everyone on.

In fact I had seriously thought about changing the midfield and putting Jerry Guscott out on the wing. However I was concerned that there would be too many alterations going on and that we could lose our shape and focus entirely. It already looked as if Gregor Townsend would be out, which turned out to be the case, and also Alan Tait. There was a danger of fragmenting all the good work, so we stuck with Jerry and Scott Gibbs.

We were not able to nail down selection until Thursday, what with all the injuries and the fatigue. The game at Welkom could easily have been written off as an irrelevance. On this tour, though, every last detail counted. It was a tougher encounter in some ways than anticipated. These up-country games were the norm in 1974. There are so few opportunities now for getting away from the main beat. It is understandable but a shame. It was a big day for the town and they laid on a real show. I know that Fran was moved to criticise the referee and the hard pitch afterwards, but in terms of hospitality and warmth of welcome the host union could not be faulted. You could see how much it meant to the local community who helped erect all the marquees around the ground.

The game was physical but to my mind not

Jason Leonard on the receiving end of a Northern Free State boot in a highly physical game.

that dirty. The referee did let them get away with murder on offside and killing the ball. Strict refereeing is so important because players can get injured or it can all boil over. I know Ollie Redman was particularly upset, which is not like him at all. We scored some cracking tries early in the game but lost concentration horribly when the referee was at his worst and let them come right back at us on the scoreboard. We were 43–12 at half-time but spoilt our record when they scored a late rush of points to finish 67–39.

We took notice though of the good points. Mark Regan came through to win the Test spot ahead of Barry Williams. Mark could easily have let his head drop when he missed out on being on the Test bench. But he did not. He trained

harder and worked to correct the weaker areas of his game. His trailing of the ball-carrier and

Simon Shaw powers his way over the line in the final mid-week game of the tour.

coming off-line were not as slick and subtle as we wanted. But Ronnie listened and he learned. His throwing was a bit quicker and more direct, too. It was very hard on Barry, a very talented hooker.

Neil Back was chosen to play instead of Richard Hill. We had been here many times on the field. His sidefooted kick which lead to John Bentley's try against Western Province was incredibly perceptive. Both he and Neil are superb at summing up a situation in an instant. Neil had battled through the bad times. It was said that he had failed at international level in the few opportunities he had had. Jim and I

Another impressive display by Neil Back secured a place in the side for the final Test.

this particular selection. Neil deserved his chance. Richard was carrying an injury, too, and did not train until Thursday. We were hell-bent on playing our wide game in the Test so it made sense to have Neil's full fitness and marvellous support. We were very fortunate in having two genuine No.7s in the ranks. Richard is not always given due credit for his awareness round

looked at the videos carefully. It seemed to me that he had not failed simply because he had not been given the chance to show what he has to offer. He had been used badly. If you play Neil Back you need to play in a certain way, the way the Lions were playing. You should in fact be aiming to make him a star, because the more he is in the game the more your game is right. If

(Left) The sides line up before the final Test.

he is not in the game then it is not his fault but ours as coaches for not creating the right playing environment.

The side was announced on Thursday. We had five players unavailable for selection through injury – Keith Wood, Jason Leonard, Gregor Townsend, Kyran Bracken and Alan Tait. We only had a short but intense session that day, only an hour and twenty minutes including warm-up and down. That was all that was needed. It was going to be a very stiff call on Saturday no matter what shape we had been in. I had seen that with the All Blacks the year before. Teams do not win at Ellis Park unless they are absolutely spot-on. The Springboks, who had made six changes in all, had never been whitewashed in an official series. There was little need to emphasise to the players that the Springboks would have their eyeballs out on Saturday. They had seen it all for themselves at close range.

Mind you, I did not think the Boks were taking us for granted either. They knew that we had not managed to put our wide game into operation and that we would want to sign off in that vein. They knew too that we could inflict our own physical damage on them. The tackling of Scott Gibbs – particularly the hits in different games on two of their mountainous props, le Roux and du Randt – had made him into a cult figure. I cannot say often enough how much we benefited from the input of the Rugby League boys. They talked all the time, aligning and re-aligning, encouraging and intimidating. Every time Honiball tried to muscle through he would be flattened by Scott who shouted at him to come again as often as he pleased because he would always be there waiting.

And so to the final Test. It was so strange. We had far more of the game than in the previous two Tests, yet lost. It was easy to see why. We had nothing like the same levels of concentration and self-discipline. We missed chances to put them away, opportunities which we had been ruthless in taking throughout the tour. We gave away far more penalties than normal, lost our cool on a couple of occasions, and allowed them to relieve pressure or kick for goal. I am convinced that if we had had to win that match then we would have won it; that if we had needed to be 100 per cent focused and bent on victory that we would have come through. Easy to say, I know, but all the evidence from the rest of the tour suggests that it is true.

We had a golden opportunity in the very first minute. There was a good forward drive from a line out, the ball went wide to Jerry who then threw a wayward pass which they hacked upfield. Jerry had never done that before on the tour. He would have realised in other games the need to take it in or someone would have found him to run off at an angle. Little things but big consequences. I cannot criticise the players, really, because the intent was there. It was just that the execution was that bit off-line.

De Beer, who had been brought in at fly half instead of Honiball, kicked two early goals. Then we took our eye off the ball thinking the referee, Wayne Erickson, had signalled for an infringement. He certainly made to raise his arm but even so we should not have stopped as Montgomery strolled over for a try. Suddenly it was 13–0 and we were right up against it. It was this five per cent loss of attention which thwarted so much of what we did. We kept the ball in hand far more than in Cape Town or Durban but lacked precise shape and definition.

(Main picture) Joost van der Westhuizen slips through the tackle of Neil Jenkins to score his third try of the series.
(Left) Jannie de Beer was brought in for the final Test at the expense of Honiball.
(Right) Percy Montgomery has a clear run in to the line to give the Springboks a commanding lead.
(Far right) Joost van der Westhuizen points the way to the Johannesburg crowd.

We got too flat, played too wide and so became too one-dimensional. It was simply that we were too tired to get into the positions we needed to, to keep working off the ball-carrier until the field really opened up. We had more possession this time, a tribute to the pack. Tom Smith had his best game of the tour.

out of defence, and looked sharp and positive. However he just could not get a pass away and turned in again. If only ... the usual sporting cry in the wake of defeat. But it was so heartening to see us go for it because unless the players have that frame of mind under pressure than we will never change our habits in the northern

Allan Bateman. a replacement for the injured Jeremy Guscott, tries to break through the tackle of Henry Honiball.

We were very close to playing outstandingly well. There were two very good try-scoring chances missed in the second half. Allan Bateman, who had come on at half-time for Jeremy Guscott, made one scintillating break

hemisphere. The psychological attitude is the key to moving the game forward. We have all got to want to play this way because it is the only way ultimately to succeed.

I was not too worried even when the score

went to 23–9. As long as we were creating, then we were in with a shout. We all knew that because it had been that way in the other two Tests. Neil Jenkins had done his stuff as usual to get us to 13–9 at half-time but then we let van der Westhuizen in for a try. Matt Dawson let him slip out of his grasp and over he went. It was a

they could feel the Springboks rocking. They could sense that panic was setting in, the thought that here come the Lions again with a late charge. But we did not kill them off this time. Those chances slipped by and the Boks hit us hard in the closing moments. Those last five to six minutes were very tough indeed. They

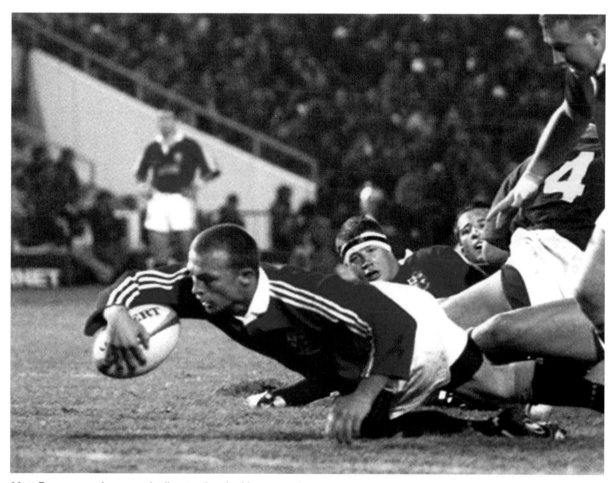

Matt Dawson reaches over the line to give the Lions some hope.

repeat scenario of so many of their tries – miss the tackle and they are in. Matt made amends when he did the same fifteen minutes from time, lunging over from close range. That made it 23–16 and the players told me afterwards that

were always going to score those two tries if they ran hard. I thought Pieter Rossouw on the Springbok left wing played really well. He set up one try and scored the other himself to make it 35–16.

Ian McGeechan, Martin Johnson and Fran Cotton parade the trophy after their 2–1 series win.

I was disappointed at the final whistle. I did not think the scoreboard reflected the run of play but they had been saying the same thing seven days earlier. The team got into a huddle at the centre circle, the subs and the rest of the squad quickly followed. That was it. The initial dismay was soon gone, for this was the moment to celebrate a unique achievement. Luckily it had been decided only a week before to award a trophy for the series, the Lion Challenge, named after the sponsoring South African brewery rather than ourselves. It meant that there was something tangible to focus on, that we could shed the immediate disappointment of the lost match and reflect on the whole series. Martin Johnson went up for the Cup and then they all went around the pitch for a well-merited lap of honour.

Martin Johnson becomes only the third captain this century to lead his team to a series victory in South Africa.

Time to party for the Lions.

What they said after the third Test

Martin Johnson: *At 23--16 we had a chance and didn't take it. Last week we took our chances, this week we didn't. They finished stronger, which is something we have prided ourselves on but we couldn't pull it out today. It shows how good our defence was, to have kept them out the last two weeks. We tried to dig deep but we couldn't manage it. It has been a long tour, something like a ten and a half month season, and we're very tired. But this is the culmination of a great squad effort and at no stage has any member of the party let the tour down. They can all be proud of themselves.*

Fran Cotton: *The Springboks deserved to win. We arrived here with three objectives. The first was to win the series, which we have. The second was to offer spectators some enjoyable rugby to watch, and I think we've managed that, and the third was to enjoy South Africa, and how could you not enjoy such a beautiful country? In my view this is a very important moment in the development of British and Irish rugby.*

Jim Telfer: *South Africa finished off very well. What we failed to do in the second half was to be more direct. We were playing too much across the field and their defence was very well fanned out. We might have taken it through the middle more but that was the best we have played in the three Tests. The forwards played very well, they were very tight in all aspects of play. The players are getting better and better – it's a pity we're going home and we we'll never play again.*

Mark Regan: *We didn't find it too difficult to hold the Springboks in the scrums but there was just so much running – that was far harder than any international I've played in at home.*

Carel du Plessis: *That was an important win for us. The team knew it had the makings and the backs were under a lot of pressure to perform. It was good to see them come through. They had to prove themselves as individuals and collectively. The Tri-Nations will be a different proposition but some of the younger players have been in a Test now, they had to go out and produce under pressure, they have done well and we must build on that.*

What lessons have we learned? That you have to have a goal-kicker in your team. If you have the opportunity to score points you must take it and put points on the board. We are still looking to create tries and score them, I'm not prepared to move away from that, but at the same time we need to win Test matches. You can't allow a top-level team like the Lions back into the game by not using your opportunities. I would rate the Lions amongst the top four sides in the world, along with New Zealand, Australia and South Africa.

Joost van der Westhuizen: *We have learned a lot from the series. The Lions surprised us all although today we wanted to win by a huge margin, and that's what we did. Everyone in South Africa expected the Lions to play slow, the usual northern-hemisphere game, but they surprised us all with their handling skills and taking the ball forward. The Lions are in the top class at the moment but I would expect the All Blacks to have the edge – they make fewer mistakes and provide quicker loose ball.*

Louis Luyt: *The Lions have played like men, like true rugbymen. I said at the start that I have never seen a bad Lions side and I meant it. We want to see the red jerseys here more often.*

International Teamwork

*Whatever position you play in,
we're with you
right down the line*

Scottish Life

the **PENSION** company

Scottish Life

International

TL TIMELIFE
INSURANCE

Meet David.

David's investments used to be (un)managed by David, until he asked for some expert help.

David has spent a lifetime acquiring shares and opening savings accounts, and would be the first to describe his portfolio as "a bit of a mixed bag, to be honest." Which is why David asked about Midland Private Banking, a service that gives each of its customers a dedicated manager to manage their portfolio of stocks and shares. The managers can offer independent advice on pensions, trusts, wills and investments; they will handle all the administration; they can even do your tax returns. If – like David – you don't pay enough attention to your finances and would like to have someone who does, and you've got savings and investments of over one hundred thousand pounds call 0800 180 180 for a brochure.

Midland Private Banking

Member HSBC *Group*

He called
0800 180 180
for a brochure.

Pick up the phone,

or cut the coupon.

Mr/Mrs/Ms/other _____ Full Name _____

Address _____

Town _____ County _____

Postcode _____ Telephone _____

Midland Private Banking Customer Information, PO Box 757, Hemel Hempstead HP2 4SS.

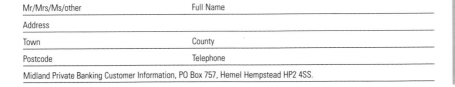

7. A TEAM EFFORT

And so began a long session of celebration. The boys had kept themselves in check for two months. They deserved every last minute of that weekend's fun. I think I topped the sleeping charts at about three hours. Several of the guys went straight through to the Sunday afternoon party organised by our sponsors. There was a bar near the hotel in the northern suburbs of Johannesburg where we all gathered for the usual cocktail of drink, food and music. It was good to see nearly all the players there. It was not a formal gathering at all. The press came along, there were some locals who just happened to be there and the whole place swung for a few hours. I genuinely believe that they all enjoyed each other's company which massively helped us to mould together so quickly.

It had been such a magnificent experience. There was hardly anything out of kilter. The

Jim Telfer, pictured here with Jason Leonard, was Ian McGeechan's first choice as assistant coach.

relationship with Jim Telfer, as I knew, had clicked into place immediately. If I could choose any other coach in the world to work with it would be Jim every time. It is not just that he can get stuck into the forwards while I do the rest. It is more than that, we are on exactly the same wavelength. We are chalk and cheese in many respects in character but there is scarcely a speck of difference in our rugby outlooks. Fair play to Fran in this regard. He asked me who I wanted to be assistant coach and I said: 'Jim Telfer.' He was not on the Home Unions' list of nominations but Fran went to them and insisted that I had my way. There were some rumblings in committee apparently but Fran won the day.

The Home Unions were, by and large, very supportive. My only quibble with them had come over the original idea for a tour bonus payment. They wanted the £5,000 bonus to be paid only for winning three Tests. I said that was crazy. It had never been done in the history of the game. I felt there ought to be an incentive for winning just one Test. The compromise was that the bonus was paid for a series victory. The players, in fact, never once mentioned money which is rare in the extreme these days. They had eyes only on the sporting goal itself. For my part I think we undervalued the Lions in pure financial terms. A fee of £10,000 plus the bonus does not equate with what was achieved by professional sportsmen. This is not a major beef but simply an observation about the need to set the correct value on what is being undertaken. A tour such as this ought to be worth in the region of £30,000.

Fran was a good man to have alongside. He had so much in place before we even left the UK that it made the coaching itself out in South Africa that much easier. It was the most intense tour I have ever been on but the actual quality time available was that much better. In Australia there were just five of us on the management team so you had to do everything yourself. Here there were twelve. Fran fought for that in committee and got it. On the tour itself there were very few flash-points – the Bosman incident, Scott Gibbs's suspension and the last provincial match at Northern Free State where Fran lost his cool. We had eyes only for the job in hand and had taken a policy decision not to get distracted. It worked perfectly. As Jim Telfer put it, as only he can; 'Managers manage, coaches coach and players play.'

Andy Keast was a huge bonus for us. We wanted someone to assist in the technical preparation. It was Martin Bayfield who first mentioned Andy's name to me. Before joining Quins as assistant coach, Andy had been with Natal for two years so would have first-hand insight into so many of their top players. Harlequins were also using a computer programme to help their video analysis. I had a word with Dick Best, then director of rugby at Quins and who had been my assistant coach in 1993, and that was it. Andy was one of the unsung heroes of the tour. He saved me hour upon hour in the video room. It was not just the time he put in either, which was considerable, it was knowing that there was quality input to the whole operation. It meant that you came to team meetings knowing for certain that the work had been done and that it was meaningful work. The players all had individual tapes prepared for them too, on their own game and

Fran Cotton looks on at a training session, whilst Andy Keast (inset) provided great technical experience.

that of their opponents. I cannot praise Andy too highly. I know he must have been frustrated at not getting on to the training pitch itself too often because he is a first-rate coach in his own right. As it was, he would come out of his room gasping for fresh air. He was an excellent choice.

So too was Dave Alred, the kicking coach, who was an eleventh hour call-up. Again it was Fran's pleading in committee which swung the financial decision in our favour. Was it worth it?

How much value do you put on winning a Test series? As it turned out, our goal-kicking was one of the fundamental differences between the teams. When it mattered, in provincial games too, we kicked our goals. We coped with that pressure; the Springboks did not. Dave was another piece of the jigsaw. We harped on about this being the first professional tour and here was proof. Dave gave us something which I could not provide and which the players could not manage as well on their own. Dave would have done a two-hour kicking session if we had let him. He is that enthusiastic and that meticulous. As it was we gave him little but often, twenty-minute stints at every opportunity. He made the kickers focus and think about their roles all over the pitch. Jenks was world-class anyway but consider that Tim Stimpson finished with one more point than he did for the tour (111 pts) and you can assess Dave's contribution. Consider also the precision of Matt Dawson's kicking from the base in the Test matches. It was spot-on but only because he had spent hour after hour on the training field with Dave. It was a case of the old Gary Player maxim – the more I practise the luckier I get.

The whole medical set-up was outstanding. James Robson, as I have mentioned, is the best sports doctor I have come across. Quite why the Scottish Rugby Union do not use him more is beyond me. He has a first-rate medical mind, is a trained physio and also a good man-manager. It is easy to get too close to players, to lose your objectivity because you are too friendly and too sympathetic. James got the balance spot on. Early in the tour a few players were slack in turning up for treatment or a change of strapping. James let them know straight away that it was not good enough. He helped to get

Scott Gibbs back on tour within seven days when he damaged his ankle and, as we have seen, he effectively saved Will Greenwood's life. When he was appointed, James then chose his own support staff. Mark Davies was a last-minute substitute for Kevin Murphy, tour physiotherapist for England and the Lions for so many years. Kevin withdrew over a financial wrangle with the Home Unions who would not fund the cover needed for his practice. I must say I think they got it wrong. The work is invaluable. 'Smurf' has proved that before; Mark Davies carried on in that vein.

Richard Wegrzyk was the masseur, a new addition to a tour party. Again it was a tip from the All Blacks which prompted me to request one. The need to recover quickly is paramount on a tour as compact and intense as this. So too is the urge to feel relaxed. Richard's fingers worked overtime. He was an acupuncturist as well which helped get so much stress out of the body.

Dave McLean was the fitness advisor which was a slight understatement of his role. He was responsible for the whole well-being of the squad, a brief which covered everything from diet, gauging rest and sleep patterns to anxiety management and also, of course, physical fitness itself. Dave took most of the warm-up sessions but his real input came with his evaluations of how the players were coping. He monitored their recovery the day after games at the local Health and Racquets Clubs where they would swim or take saunas. Dave also worked on the players's body-fat levels. This was a healthy squad when they congregated but Dave managed to engineer an average two per cent reduction of body fat across the party. The measure of his work was that, three weeks into the tour, no one was mentioning one of the real pre-tour fears; that is, that we would be too tired to compete after such an arduous season.

Stan Bagshaw, the baggage master, had a huge logistical exercise to contend with. He had to shift three tons of baggage around the country. He also had the unwholesome task of sorting out the players' laundry, of making sure that what needed to be washed was left out for washing. Stan was on hand, too, to help lay out the dressing-rooms before the players arrived. It was all rather unglamorous but vital nonetheless.

Finally a word for our Lioness, Sam Peters, the only woman among the entire squad. Sam was the administrative assistant which meant that she had to ensure that all the logistics were in good order and that hotel accounts were correct and settled. She also liaised with the media. She was an absolute gem. Sam is only in her mid-twenties but was so mature in that she was so natural. She got on with her job, made no fuss, no big announcements and quickly earned the respect of everyone. She worked closely with Jonathan Goslett, the South African liaison man. He was superb too. Nothing was ever too much trouble.

All that was left on the Monday morning was somehow to take in everything, to try and appreciate what we had been through. It would soon be gone. That was both the beauty and the sadness of the Lions experience. I so hope that the legacy will live on in the rugby played over this forthcoming season. I am convinced it is the way forward but it will take courage for the coaches to put it into action. So much has to change. The whole ethos and practice are different. Our lines of running go right against the coaching manual. The textbook says run straight: the Lions ran off-line. For that to happen effectively, so much else has to happen

around. The ball-carrier has to trust in the support around him whereas the support runner has to read the body-language of the man in front to know where he is going. It is a philosophy of reactive play, deciding in an instant the correct option and knowing that those around will be reading only your body language to make their own decisions. The whole intention is to be unstructured in a structured way, to go where the opposition cannot anticipate you being and so cannot find you. We were just not interested in set-piece moves done by numbers. It was the exact opposite of that outlook. From day one we worked with each other and for each other so that we could play it our way. Everything we did from that first session was geared to beating the Springboks. As it happened, we won all but one of the provincial games too, but that opposition was never our principal concern. We were concentrating every last aspect into beating South Africa. And we did it.

We all went to the airport together. It was strange to think of the England boys heading on down to Australia. I do not think any of us envied them. Three of them, Martin Johnson, Jason Leonard and Jeremy Guscott, were coming back with us to be treated for various ailments. It was fitting that Johnno should lead the party home. He had been a first-rate skipper, fulfilling every last little bit of the role I envisaged. We wanted a flat management structure throughout with no false hierarchies. Martin was perfect. He has no side to him, no ego at all. Look at how much ball he called for Jeremy Davidson in the Tests. He knew that the Boks had probably worked a strategy to block him so he sent the ball elsewhere. He was not the least bit concerned about how it would look for him. He battled through with his groin complaint, which needed an operation when he got home. He also dislocated a shoulder joint early in the tour which we managed to keep relatively quiet. All in all, Martin Johnson, in his own understated way, was a superb captain.

It was hard now for we all knew it was over. We had a little ceremony at the airport. But you soon saw the England boys drift off to gather their stuff for the flight to Sydney. We had a great send-off from Virgin whose staff had all volunteered specially to be on our flight to London. They did not run out of drink, which was a huge achievement. It was one hell of a party, two of the boys, Neil Jenkins and Jeremy Guscott, being presented with birthday cakes.

Someone asked me about the next Lions tour in 2001. There is no way I could beat what I have just been through. It is an enormous privilege to have had three shots, as it is. I have toured all three southern-hemisphere countries so that is it. It has been a fantastic adventure. The magic of this particular experience was best summed up by Nigel Redman. Who could have imagined Ollie leading the Lions out at Bloemfontein? We all have different dreams and they do sometimes come true. They did for Ollie. And they did for me too.

Transport was never a problem thanks to Land Rover who provided a fleet of vehicles at all the main centres.

Midland Bank congratulates Martin Johnson, captain of the 1997 British Lions

Midland Bank

Member HSBC *Group*

8. TOUR REFLECTIONS

After the third Test BBC rugby correspondent Ian Robertson spoke to Lions captain, Martin Johnson, and to tour manager, Fran Cotton. He also got a South African view of the series from their 1995 World Cup coach, Kitch Christie.

MARTIN JOHNSON

The Lions could hardly have made a worse start to the first Test with so much going wrong in the first five minutes. Were you worried at that stage?

I was disappointed rather than worried because we made mistakes rather than the Springboks doing anything particularly good. I mean we kicked the ball straight out from the kick-off, lost the scrum and when they belted the ball down the field we then lost the line out. But in that dreadful sequence the only worry I had was the first scrum. They charged at us, hit us really hard and drove us back, and I knew if we were not solid in the scrums it would be very hard to win the match. The next couple of scrums were just as bad with us under pressure and the referee giving South Africa a penalty which they kicked to take the lead. But then at the fourth scrum everything settled down. Our front row packed low and we put into practice everything that Jim Telfer and Ian McGeechan had been working on since we were outscrummaged by Western Province early on in the tour. Thanks to the countless hours of hard work we had put into scrummaging and the technical expertise we had acquired, we not only held our own in the first and second Tests we actually dominated and controlled the scrums. We didn't really push the Springboks backwards but we were able to wheel them, which had a negative effect for them on their ball and gave us a positive advantage on our ball. So once we were ten minutes into the first Test I was confident we would do well because we were comfortable in the set pieces.

How did you react at half-time when you were leading 9–8?

I told the team we had made quite a few mistakes in the first half and we had spent a lot of time in our own half of the field which cut down our attacking opportunities but we still were in the lead, so with a really big effort the game was there for the taking. We all knew the team spirit was phenomenal and there was no shortage of confidence, and we received a fantastic inspiration from the huge defensive effort of the whole team. It must have been very dispiriting for the Springboks to throw everything at us in a bruising physical forward battle of attrition and to find we relished the opportunity to knock them backwards in the tackle over and over again. They must have expected us to crack at some point but we never did. It was a truly magnificent defensive rearguard effort in the first and second Tests which the Springboks must have found extremely frustrating. From the Lions' point of view it was just an unforgettable experience to be part of a team utterly determined never to take a step backwards, never to miss a tackle and above all never to let our teammates down.

Was there, in your view, a turning point in each of the first two Tests when you felt this was the moment the match was won?

In simple terms I knew we were going to win the moment Matt Dawson sprinted off down the blind side for his try in the first Test and similarly when Jerry Guscott dropped his goal in the second Test. They were the actual moments I knew we were going to win but the feeling of confidence that we were on top in both Tests came in all sorts of ways. We were not just comfortable in the scrums, we were in control of the scrums. We had no trouble in winning our own line-out ball. In defence they were very predictable and we were totally focused. In all three Tests our back division looked far more dangerous than theirs. So though there were two specific moments of pure genius from Dawson and Guscott which actually clinched each Test, it was a combination of a variety of other factors which meant I was pretty confident in both Tests we had a really great chance of winning.

How impressive did you feel the Lions tackling was? Have you played in an international when a team's defence was better?

No, I don't think I have. I think our defence in the first two Tests was outstanding by any standards. The loose forwards made the first hits, but the front five also slotted in a lot of tackles and there was some tremendous tackling in midfield especially by Scott Gibbs. The most important thing was the speed of our tackling. We hardly let them cross the gain line even from rucks and mauls and we were so aggressive and forthright we continually slowed them down and took the sting out of them. All credit to Ian McGeechan, he told us what would happen and he devised a series of short, sharp sessions which concentrated on our defensive skills and organisation. We went into those first two Tests in the right frame of mind, totally focused and every player knowing exactly what his role was and what we had to do as a team. We were 100 per cent prepared and it paid off. What was so good was that in the second half of those Tests, when we were tired and really hurting, every single player responded in the same way because they knew what they had to do – dig deep and concentrate on every tackle. It was an unbelievably rewarding experience.

Can you describe the feeling of euphoria at the final whistle in Cape Town and Durban?

To be honest, I was delighted we had won but personally I don't get massively elated at the end of a game when the whistle goes. I think my first feeling was one of relief that we had come to South Africa to win a Test series and we had

succeeded. Certainly on the Sunday after each Test I really did have a great feeling that we had achieved the near impossible and I had a huge sense of a job well done.

Would you say the first two Tests produced two of the best team efforts with which you have been associated?

Without a shadow of a doubt, those two Tests would be right up there at the top of my greatest rugby highlights. We won a similar sort of Test match with the Lions against New Zealand in 1993 which would also rank very highly and also there was immense satisfaction when England beat New Zealand at Twickenham in 1993. The Tests on this tour in Cape Town and Durban were the sort of matches that when you come off at the end and you look all your teammates in the eye you all know that every single player has done his job, that every player has played to his full potential, that in very difficult circumstances everyone has made a superhuman effort to help secure the victory. Such a collective effort is a very special feeling.

Was the third Test a bit of an anti-climax?

It was really although we tried to prepare just as well for Joburg as we did for the first two Tests. We had the Sunday off after Durban but from the Monday on I tried to keep our roll going. We knew we had a fantastic opportunity to rewrite the history books because no touring team this century had every inflicted a whitewash on the Springboks in a Test series in South Africa. But I think events conspired against us. We had a lot of illness in the camp in the last week, which had a debilitating effect, and several injuries. In the end we made six changes in our third Test team from our first Test side. You also have to remember the final Test was played on the High Veldt at 6,000 feet which certainly suits the Springboks more than the Lions. Furthermore, by the last Test, the Springboks had got their act together. As it transpired I thought we played some great rugby at Ellis Park and we were still in real contention near the end when we were only trailing 23-16, but the match slipped out of our reach. It was still a great team effort on our part and perhaps, having already won the series, we were not quite as focused as we had been for the first two Tests. At any rate the feeling of disappointment at losing was short-lived. The Lions received the trophy for winning the series and, as we held it aloft to the thousands of cheering British supporters in the crowd, we knew we had nothing to be ashamed of. Indeed we could all be very proud that we had joined a very select band of only two other sides this century who had won a Test series in South Africa. Our final message was very simple – Mission Accomplished.

The winning team – a cartoon that appeared in the programme for the final Test.

FRAN COTTON

Is it fair to say the biggest problem you had as a manager was selection of fifteen players for the first Test out of the squad of thirty-five when everyone was playing so well?

Absolutely. Initially we had expected to know our Test side before the Natal game, the Saturday before the Test, but I have to say when we sat down after the match against the Emerging Springboks the following Tuesday it was only then we really began to sort out the team. Surprisingly, it did not take all that long to sort out the front row. At the start of the tour the England front row might well have been the favourites, but by the time of the first Test we were all agreed on Smith, Wood and Wallace. Firstly, we felt they would be the best scrummaging unit and that was the most important factor against the Springboks and then we had the added bonus that we knew they would all three be pretty dynamic in the open. As it turned out, the biggest debates were at lock forward to choose a partner for Martin Johnson, the back-row combination and a centre to play alongside Jeremy Guscott. In the end after a lot of soul-searching we chose Davidson ahead of Shaw at lock, Dallaglio, Rodber and Hill and Scott Gibbs in the centre. There was also a lot of discussion about the left wing but for a variety of reasons we switched Alan Tait to that position rather than picking a recognised wing.

The victory in the Test at Cape Town vindicated this selection, didn't it?

I would go further than that and say that perhaps the big factor in our favour in Cape Town was that we picked exactly the right team for that match and the way we wanted to play. The Springboks, judging by the number of changes they made in the next two Tests, did not come up with their best side for that first Test.

Is it fair to compare the 1997 Lions with the 1974 Lions in the sense that they kept improving and they kept winning except for Northern Transvaal and the whole squad kept playing well?

From what I remember as a player in the '74 tour, the big similarity was the fact that a successful tour builds up its own momentum. We certainly did that in 1974 and the Lions did that again in 1997. The second major similarity was that on each of those Lions tours we had an outstanding Test side but we also had an outstanding midweek side. This meant the Test team had to operate at 100 per cent in every match because they were being pushed all the time by the midweek players. Thirdly, on both tours we had really top class players in the key positions which gave us a decided edge over the Springboks. And, finally, on both tours we got our Test selection absolutely right and the South Africans did not.

Was there a turning point on the tour in the build-up to the first Test which you can look back on and feel that was the moment things changed in favour of the Lions?

Yes, it was our win over the Gauteng Lions in Johannesburg. We made far too many mistakes when we lost to Northern Transvaal in a game we really should have won and I believe the defining moment of the tour came the following Wednesday when we played exceptionally well to beat Gauteng [or Transvaal as it used to be called]. That win put us back in control and then we produced an even better performance in convincingly beating Natal on the Saturday. From those two wins we went into the first Test bubbling with confidence.

Having said that, the first few minutes of the Test did not go very well. Two collapsed scrums leading to a penalty and the Lions were 3–0 down. You wouldn't have put your mortgage on the Lions winning at that point, would you?

No, we definitely did not start too well. We kicked the ball straight out, lost the scrum, then collapsed a couple and found ourselves three points down. But we put together a few very solid scrums after that, packing really low. We won our first few line outs quite easily and I felt very comfortable, especially when Neil Jenkins kicked a penalty to level the score. After the first five minutes we scrummaged much more intelligently than the Springboks and there is no doubt Ian McGeechan and Jim Telfer comprehensively outthought them. We often succeeded in wheeling them which on their ball made it very difficult for van der Westhuizen, their best back, to break at scrum half, and also on our ball it edged their loose forwards into midfield to give us more room on the blind side. It was this manoeuvre which led directly to Matt Dawson's blind-side try which helped enormously to win the first Test and the series.

The line out went well and I assume you were delighted with the performance of Jeremy Davidson?

He had a great first Test match for the Lions because Martin chose to throw to him most of the game. He won the ball cleanly and was in complete control. We also won a bit at the back and when the set-pieces are going really well it is much easier for the pack to be dynamic in the loose.

What would you say was the single most important aspect of play which helped to win that first Test?

Unquestionably our defence. The coaches had worked on this and primed the team and I have to say all fifteen players defended quite magnificently. The loose forwards rattled in the big hits for the whole eighty minutes and the claustrophobic pressure we put on their fly half ,Henry Honiball, was too much for him to handle. That greatly reduced the threat from their three-quarter line because Honiball was rendered ineffective when he dropped a little deeper and a little wider as he lost his confidence. I think we surprised the Springboks with our totally ruthless utter commitment to defence. The first Test was a great day for British Lions rugby.

So was the second Test. Is it fair to say that although the Springboks made a few changes the big change for the second Test was not in personnel but in attitude and approach?

Yes. If we thought they came at us hard in Cape Town, in Durban they threw absolutely everything at us. What really frustrated them, apart from their very poor goal-kicking, was that we took everything head-on and defended even more resolutely in the second Test than we did in the first. I can't remember a game where a team spent so much time on the offensive bombarding us up front with fierce forward-driving rugby and we took it all, defended superbly and still found the energy, character and determination to fight back and win.

They felt particularly disappointed that they outscored the Lions by three tries to none and still lost. Do they have a point?

I have no doubt they must have been very frustrated with the final scoreline, but they only have to look back two years to the month and recall how they won the World Cup final. They beat the All Blacks with a magnificent defensive performance and deadly accurate kicking from Joel Stransky culminating in the winning drop-kick. We did exactly the same – superb defence, five penalties from Neil Jenkins and a drop goal by Jerry Guscott. That sort of display was good enough for South Africa to win the World Cup in 1995 and for the Lions to win the Test series.

Would you agree the second Test was very similar to the first?

Yes, it was. They tried to win the game through the power play of their pack and when we

defended successfully against that and pressurised Honiball out of the game they didn't really have a Plan B. I have to say that simply hammering away all day with power play from the forwards is a very old-fashioned approach and it is unlikely to work at the very highest level. But make no mistake, this was another magnificent British Lions win. To put it in perspective, only three major touring sides this century have won a Test series in South Africa and that shows the magnitude of the achievement of the 1997 Lions.

What went wrong in the third Test?

I think it was just one bridge too far. We had a severely disrupted preparation with a stomach bug which affected over half the party and a few injury problems. We lost both wings in the final Test – Ieuan Evans and Alan Tait, hooker Keith Wood, No.8 Tim Rodber and our first choice fly half Gregor Townsend. Then during the match we lost Jerry Guscott with a broken arm. At 23–16 down with fifteen minutes left I thought we might do it, but at 6,000 feet altitude and with the Test series already won we just lost our concentration. It was not that we played badly, because in many ways we produced some of our best rugby of the tour, but the Springboks played well and deserved to win.

You won a Test series in South Africa as a player in 1974 and as the manager in 1997. You won a Grand Slam with England in 1980. Where does the 1997 Lions fit in your rugby highlights?

I think the greatest highlights came as a player, so 1974 would be right up there at the top but in my role as a non-player this is undoubtedly the high point of my career. To win this Test series is something very special indeed and I have been very proud and privileged to be a part of a tremendous touring party. It's been great for British and Irish rugby and a great boost for the game in the northern hemisphere.

KITCH CHRISTIE

What gave the British Lions the edge in the three Test series?

I think one big advantage the Lions had was their management team. They had such wealth of experience in their management set-up with Fran Cotton the manager and the two coaches, Ian McGeechan and Jim Telfer. All three were former British Lions themselves, with Cotton and McGeeghan two of the key men in the unbeaten 1974 Lions side and Jim Telfer just as experienced as a player in 1966 and 1968 and as the coach in 1983. Against these three men of the world, the South African management of Arthob Petersen, Carel du Plessis and Gert Smal, through no fault of their own, were in their first season of major international rugby and there is no doubt it takes a great deal of time to adjust to the difficult demands of organising and running a global outfit like the Springboks.

Arguably, the biggest single advantage the Lions had was in their coach, Ian McGeechan. Here was a man who had coached the Lions to a great Test series victory in Australia in 1989 and who came so close to repeating this triumph in New Zealand in 1993. He had two tours comprising twenty-six matches including six Tests behind him whilst the Springbok coach Carel du Plessis had never coached any senior side at any level when he was suddenly asked to coach the Springboks in an emergency situation after the previous coach André Markgraaff suddenly resigned. Carel was a great Springbok wing and could well develop into a great Springbok coach but he would be the first to admit you learn by experience in every walk of life and, compared to Ian McGeechan, he was very inexperienced.

McGeechan did an excellent job in a very short time in welding together thirty-five players from England, Scotland, Ireland and Wales into a team. In fact he welded them into two teams because once he sorted out his Test side he managed not only to keep the midweek dirt-trackers interested and keen, he produced an unbeaten side which won every single midweek match playing rugby of the highest calibre.

But perhaps McGeechan's main stroke of genius was to choose Jim Telfer to coach the forwards. I think Jim is a really outstanding forward coach and his mark was stamped all over this Lions pack from the outset. He produced a well-organised and disciplined pack to play a dynamic style of rugby and I believe there is no praise too high for him. Early on in the tour the Lions forwards were badly outscrummaged by Western Province but by the Test series they had a better scrummaging unit than the Springboks. Telfer must take the credit.

How on earth did they manage such a remarkable transformation because even on the eve of the first Test there were fears amongst the British supporters that the Lions would be destroyed in the scrums?

First of all, because the management team were three such established people they were in a position to do whatever they wanted. They had such respect in the game that they could be bold and radical and that is what they were. Instead of choosing the whole England tight five, which is what most critics expected, they had the courage to drop four of the England pack which comfortably won the Triple Crown. They went for Tom Smith and Paul Wallace at prop and decided to scrummage pretty low which, with these two shorter props, made it very difficult for the Springboks pack to drive them backwards as Western Province had done. With Keith Wood at hooker they then had not only a very solid scrum they also had three excellent mobile forwards in the loose. Nowadays with the new line-out laws it is much easier to win your own ball and so the Lions chose Ireland's Jeremy Davidson instead of England's Simon Shaw at lock. They sacrificed height at the line out but it didn't matter because Davidson won virtually all his own ball in all three Tests and he was also outstanding in the loose. It was this sort of inspirational selection which helped to win the series.

If you had to pick on one moment which turned the series the Lions way, what would it be?

For me the most important aspect was the Lions getting their scrummaging right. That gave them the base they needed and it was from a scrum they scored the try which turned the series in their favour. With ten minutes of the first Test left the Lions had a scrum about twenty-five metres out near the right touchline. They were so solid and in control at the scrum they were able through the tight head to turn the whole scrummage infield a few degrees. This automatically edged each of the Springboks loose forwards a few feet away from the touchline and a little nearer the centre of the field. They had done this a few minutes before from a similar position but Tim Rodber picked up and didn't quite have the speed to break right through. This time the scrum half, Matt Dawson, picked up and accelerated across the gain line to beat the first line of defence and he then sold a dummy to the cover before sprinting in at the corner. That put the Lions in the lead at 20–16 and helped them to win the first Test and the series.

If you had to take one area of play in the first two Tests which swung it the Lions way, what would it be?

Rather than choose just one aspect I would choose three areas which made the difference between the sides. The first we have already dealt with and that is the scrummage. Instead of being an area of weakness and concern, it was an area of strength and a springboard to a bold style of rugby during the tour. Secondly, the Lions defence right through the tour but especially in the Tests was magnificent. The Springbok forwards hammered away at them for the whole eighty minutes of all three Tests but the Lions tackled, defended and covered superbly. And thirdly, in a tactical battle they

had the edge. They seemed to know from the outset that Henry Honiball was not a natural orthodox fly half and they targeted him. They forced him to lie deeper than the Springboks would have wanted and by negating him as an attacking force they really negated the Spingboks back division. I reckon these three factors contributed most to the Lions victory in the series.

How disappointed have you been that the team you built to win the World Cup in 1995 had almost disappeared just twenty-four months later? By the third Test, only three players from the World Cup had survived.

I have to accept the game moves on and players change but I do feel the Springboks were a little hasty in disposing of a handful of key players with almost indecent haste. It takes time to build a team and if you look at the All Blacks they are able to keep experience whilst gradually introducing new blood into the squad each year. I think the Springbok selection for the Lions series fell some way short of being brilliant and tactically they were not as sharp as the Lions. Although only van der Westhuizen, du Randt and Strydom remained from the World Cup success, a few other players would have been included but for injury. Nevertheless I am disappointed that a few top-class players who were instrumental in winning the World Cup have fallen from grace.

How highly do you rate the Lions achievement?

I have to rate their performance very highly indeed. Not only did they win the Test series they played some great rugby in beating all the Super 12 sides and they were perhaps at their best against Natal, Free State and Gauteng in the provincial matches. They had a lot of good players but I would have to pay special tribute to the coach Ian McGeechan for bringing out the very best in all thirty-five players and for masterminding the Test series triumph and a very successful tour.

24.5.97 Port Elizabeth
Eastern Province Invitational XV 11 British Lions 39

Eastern Province: T van Rensburg; D Keyser, R van Jaarsveld, H le Roux, H Pedro; K Ford (R Fourie 42), C Alcock; D Saayman, G Kirsten (capt), W Enslin (W Lessing 38), K Weise, A du Preez, M Webber (M van der Merwe 44), J Greejj, S Scott-Young.

British Lions: N Jenkins; I Evans (T Underwood 67), J Guscott, W Greenwood, N Beal; G Townsend, R Howley; T Smith, K Wood (B Williams 67), J Leonard (capt), D Weir, S Shaw (J Davidson 77), L Dallaglio, R Hill, S Quinnell.

Referee: A Turner (Western Province).

Eastern Province: *Try:* Keyser. *Penalty goals:* van Rensberg 2.
British Lions: *Tries:* Guscott 2, Weir, Underwood, Greenwood. *Conversions:* Jenkins 4. *Penalty goals:* Jenkins 2.

28.5.97 East London
Border 14 British Lions 18

Border: R Bennett; K Hilton-Green, G Hetcher, K Malotana (D Maidza 42), A Claassen; G Miller, J Bradbrook; H Kok, R van Zyl (capt), D du Preez, S Botha, J Gehring, M Swart, A Fox, A Botha (D Coetzer 79).

British Lions: T Stimpson; J Bentley, A Bateman, S Gibbs (A Tait 45), T. Underwood; P Grayson, A Healey (M Dawson 54); G Rowntree, M Regan, D Young (P Wallace 68), D Weir, J Davidson, R Wainwright (capt), N Back, E Miller.

Referee: A Burger (Transvaal).

Border: *Try:* Claassen. *Penalty goals:* Miller 3.
British Lions: *Tries:* Bentley, Regan, Wainwright *Penalty goal:* Stimpson.

30.5.97 Cape Town
Western Province 21 British Lions 38

Western Province: J Swart; J Small, R Fleck, D Muir (capt) (L Koen 57-60), S Berridge; P Montgomery, S Hatley; G Pagel (T van der Linde 57), A Patterson, K Andrews, F Van Heerden, H Louw, C Krige, R Brink, A Aitken.

British Lions: T Stimpson; I Evans, A Tait (W Greenwood 72), J Guscott, J Bentley; G Townsend, R Howley; G Rowntree, B Williams, J Leonard, M Johnson (capt), S Shaw, L Dallaglio, R Hill, T Rodber.

Referee: A Schwonwinkel (Free State).

Western Province: *Tries:* Muir 2, Brink. *Conversions:* Montgomery 3.
British Lions: *Tries:* Bentley 2, Tait, Evans. *Conversions:* Stimpson 3. *Penalty goals:* Stimpson 4.

3.6.97 Witbank
Mpumalanga 14 British Lions 64

Mpumalanga: E Gericke; J Visagie, R Potgieter, G Gendall, P Nel; R van As, D van Zyl; H Swart, H Kemp, A Botha, M Bosman, E van den Berg, F Rossouw, P Joubert, T Oosthuizen (capt) (J Beukes 73).

British Lions: N Beal; I Evans, A Bateman, W Greenwood, T Underwood; N Jenkins, M Dawson; T Smith, K Wood (M Regan 52), P Wallace (D Young 73), D Weir (S Shaw 55), J Davidson, R Wainwright, N Back, T Rodber (capt).

Referee: C Spannenberg (Western Province).

Mpumalanga: *Tries:* Joubert 2. *Conversions:* van As 2.
British Lions: *Tries:* Wainwright 3, Underwood 2, Evans 2, Dawson, Jenkins, Beal. *Conversions:* Jenkins 7.

7.6.97 Pretoria
Northern Transvaal 35 British Lions 30

Northern Transvaal: G Bouwer; W Lourens (G Esterhuizen 33), J Schutte, D van Schalkwyk, C Steyn; R de Marigny, C Breydenbach; L Campher, H Tromp (J Brooks h-t), P Boer (J Tajaard 71), D Grobbelaar (G Laufs 38), D Badenhorst (R Schroeder 65), N Van der Wait, S Bekker, A Richter (capt).

British Lions: T Stimpson; J Bentley (S Gibbs 59), J Guscott, A Tait, T Underwood; G Townsend, R Howley; G Rowntree, M Regan, J Leonard (D Young 74), M Johnson (capt), S Shaw, L Dallaglio, E Miller, S Quinnell.

Referee: A Watson (E Transvaal).

Northern Transvaal: *Tries*: van Schalkwyk 2, Steyn, Richter. *Conversions*: Steyn 3. *Penalty goals*: Steyn 3.
British Lions: *Tries*: Guscott 2, Townsend. *Conversions*: Stimpson 3. *Penalty goals*: Stimpson 3.

11.6.97 Johannesburg
Gauteng Lions 14 British Lions 20

Gauteng Lions: D du Toit; J Gillingham, J van der Walt, H le Roux, P Hendricks; L van Rensburg, J Roux; R Grau, C Rossouw (J Dalton 52), K van Greuning (B Swart 60), K Wiese (capt), B Thorne, A Vos, P Kreuse, W Brosnihan.

Britsh Lions: N Beal; J Bentley, J Guscott, W Greenwood, T Underwood (N Jenkins 57); M Catt, A Healey; T Smith, B Williams, P Wallace, N Redman, J Davidson, R Wainwright, N Back, T Rodber (capt).

Referee: T. Henning (N Transvaal).

Guateng Lions *Try*: Vos. *Penalty goals*: du Toit 3.
British Lions: *Tries*: Healey, Bentley. *Conversions*: Jenkins 2. *Penalty goals*: Catt, Jenkins.

14.6.97 Durban
Natal 12 British Lions 42

Natal: G Lawless; S Payne, J Thomson, P Muller, J Joubert; H Scriba, R du Preez; A-H le Roux, J Allan, R Kempson, N Wegner, J Slade, W van Heerden (R Strewwick 6-10), W Fyvie (capt), D Kriese.

British Lions: N Jenkins; I Evans, A Bateman (M Catt 65), S Gibbs, A Tait; G Townsend, R Howley (M Dawson 13); T Smith (J Leonard 67), K Wood, D Young, M Johnson (capt) (R Wainwright 26-32), S Shaw, L Dallaglio, R Hill, E Miller.

Referee: J Meuwesen (Eastern Province).

Natal: *Penalty goals*: Lawless 4.
British Lions: *Tries*: Townsend, Catt, Dallaglio. *Conversions*: Jenkins 3. *Dropped goal*: Townsend. *Penalty goals*: Jenkins 6.

17.6.97 Wellington
Emerging Springboks 22 British Lions 51

Emerging Springboks: MJ Smith (K Malotana 65); D Keyser, P Montgomery, M Hendricks, P Treu; L van Rensburg (M Goosen 22), J Adlam (K Myburgh 11); R Kempson (L Campher 68), D Santon, N du Toit, B Els, R Opperman, W Brosnihan, P Smit, J Coetzee.

British Lions: T Stimpson; N Beal, A Bateman, W Greenwood, J Bentley; M Catt, A Healey; G Rowntree, M Regan, J Leonard (capt), N Redman, J Davidson, R Wainwright, N Back, A Diprose.

Referee: I Rogers (Natal).

Emerging Springboks: *Tries*: Brosnihan, Goosen, Treu. *Conversions*: Smith, Montgomery. *Penalty goal*: Smith
British Lions: *Tries*: Beal 3, Rowntree, Stimpson, Catt. *Conversions*: Stimpson 6. *Penalty goals*: Stimpson 3.

21.6.97 Newlands, Cape Town
SOUTH AFRICA 16 BRITISH ISLES 25

South Africa: A Joubert; J Small, J Mulder, E Lubbe (R Bennett 40), A Snyman; H Honiball, J van der Westhuizen; O du Randt, N Drotske, A Garvey, H Strydom, M Andrews, R Kruger, A Venter, G Teichmann (capt).

British Isles: N Jenkins; I Evans, S Gibbs, J Guscott, A Tait; G Townsend, M Dawson; T Smith (J Leonard 79), K Wood, P Wallace, M Johnson (capt), J Davidson, L Dallaglio, R Hill, T Rodber.

Referee: C Hawke (New Zealand).

South Africa: *Tries*: du Randt, Bennett. *Penalty goals*: Lubbe, Honiball.
British Isles: *Tries*: Dawson, Tait. *Penalty goals*: Jenkins 5

24.6.97 Bloemfontein
Free State 30 British Lions 52

Free State: MJ Smith; J van Wyk, H Muller (capt), B Venter, S Brink; J de Beer, S Fourie (H Jacobs 40); D Groenewald, C Marais, W Meyer (D Heymans 60), R Opperman, B Els, C van Rensburg, J Erasmus, J Coetzee.

British Lions: T Stimpson; J Bentley, A Bateman, W Greenwood (N Jenkins 40), T Underwood; M Catt, A Healey; G Rowntree (J Leonard 16-20, 73), B Williams, D Young, N Redman (capt), S Shaw, R Wainwright, N Back, E Miller.

Referee: J Kaplan (Natal).

Free State: *Tries*: Brink 2, de Beer. *Conversions*: de Beer 3. *Penalty goals*: de Beer 3.
British Lions: *Tries*: Bentley 3, Stimpson, Bateman, Jenkins, Underwood. *Conversions*: Stimpson 4. *Penalty goals*: Stimpson 3.

28.6.97 King's Park, Durban
SOUTH AFRICA 15 BRITISH ISLES 18

South Africa: A Joubert; A Snyman, P Montgomery, D van Schalkwyk, P Rossouw; H Honiball, J van der Westhuizen; O du Randt, N Drotske, A Garvey (D Theron 67), H Strydom, M Andrews, R Kruger (F van Heerden 50), A Venter, G Teichmann (capt) (F Van Heerden 3-5).

British Isles: N Jenkins; I Evans, S Gibbs, J Guscott, A Tait (A Healey 76); G Townsend, M Dawson; T Smith, K Wood, P Wallace, M Johnson (capt), J Davidson, L Dallaglio, R Hill (N Back 57), T Rodber (E Miller 76).

Referee: D Mené (France).

South Africa: *Tries*: van der Westhuizen, Joubert, Montgomery.
British Isles: *Penalty goals*: Jenkins 5. *Dropped goal*: Guscott.

1.7.97 Welkom
Northern Free State 39 British Lions 67

Northern Free State: M Ehrentraut (J Burrows 66); R Harmse, A van Burren, T de Beer, W Nagel; E Herbert, J Jerling (capt); K Appelgryn, O Wagener, B Nell, K Heydenrich, S Nieuweuhuyzen, H Kershaw, E Delport (A Michau 75), M Venter

British Lions: T Stimpson; T Stanger, N Beal, A Bateman, T Underwood; M Catt, K Bracken (A Healey 54); J Leonard (capt) (G Rowntree 40), M Regan, D Young, N Redman, S Shaw, R Wainwright, N Back, A Diprose

Referee: D de Villiers (Western Province).

Northern Free State *Tries:* pen try, Ehrentraut, Wagener, van Buuren, Herbert. *Conversions:* Herbert 4. *Penalty goals:* Herbert 2.
British Lions: *Tries:* Underwood 3, Shaw 2, Stimpson 2, Back, Bracken, Regan. *Conversions:* Stimpson 7. *Penalty goal:* Stimpson.

5.7.97 Ellis Park, Johannesburg
SOUTH AFRICA 35   BRITISH ISLES 16

South Africa: R Bennett; A Snyman, P Montgomery (H Honiball 53), D van Schalwyk, P Rossouw; J de Beer (J Swart 71), J van der Westhuizen (W Swanepoel 81); O du Randt (A Garvey 63), J Dalton (N Drotské 69), D Theron, H Strydom, K Otto, A Venter, J Erasmus, G Teichmann (capt) (F van Heerden 73).

British Isles: N Jenkins; J Bentley, J Guscott (A Bateman 40), S Gibbs, T Underwood (T Stimpson 30); M Catt, M Dawson (A Healey 81); T Smith, M Regan, P Wallace, M Johnson (capt), J Davidson, R Wainwright, N Back, L Dallaglio.

Referee: W Erickson (Australia).

South Africa: *Tries:* Montgomery, van der Westhuizen, Snyman, Rossouw. *Conversions:* de Beer 2, Honiball. *Penalty goals:* de Beer 2.
British Isles: *Try:* Dawson. *Conversion:* Jenkins. *Penalty goals:* Jenkins 3.

TOUR SUMMARY

Played 13   Won 11   Lost 2
Points for 480   Points against 278

Tries 56. Conversions 40.
Penalty goals 38. Dropped goals 2.

Points scorers:

111	T Stimpson
110	N Jenkins
35	J Bentley, T Underwood
23	J Guscott
20	N Beal, R Wainwright
15	M Dawson, I Evans
13	G Townsend
5	N Back, A Bateman, K Bracken, L Dallaglio, W Greenwood, A Healey, G Rowntree, D Weir.

Number of appearances:
(+ = replacement)

			Total	Tests
J Bentley	Newcastle	England	8	2
N Back	Leicester	England	7+1	1+1
J Davidson	London Irish	Ireland	7+1	3
N Jenkins	Pontypridd	Wales	7+1	3
T Underwood	Newcastle	England	7+1	1
R Wainwright	Watsonians	Scotland	7+1	1
J Leonard	Harlequins	England	6+2	0+1
L Dallaglio	Wasps	England	7	3
J Guscott	Bath	England	7	3
T Smith	Watsonians	Scotland	7	3
A Bateman	Richmond	Wales	6+1	0+1
A Healey	Leicester	England	4+3	0+2
S Shaw	Bristol	England	6+1	0
T Stimpson	Newcastle	England	6+1	0+1
M Johnson	Leicester	England	6	3
G Townsend	Northampton	Scotland	6	2
M Catt	Bath	England	5+1	1
S Gibbs	Swansea	Wales	5+1	3
W Greenwood	Leicester	England	5+1	0
M Regan	Bristol	England	5+1	1
G Rowntree	Leicester	England	5+1	0
A Tait	Newcastle	Scotland	5+1	2
P Wallace	Saracens	Ireland	5+1	3
M Dawson	Northampton	England	4+2	3
D Young	Cardiff	Wales	4+2	0
N Beal	Northampton	England	5	0
I Evans	Llanelli	Wales	5	1
R Hill	Saracens	England	5	2
T Rodber	Northampton	England	5	2
K Wood	Harlequins	Ireland	5	2
E Miller	Leicester	Ireland	4+1	0+1
R Howley	Cardiff	Wales	4	0
N Redman	Bath	England	4	0
B Williams	Richmond	Wales	3+1	0
D Weir	Newcastle	Scotland	3	0
S Quinnell	Richmond	Wales	2+1	0
A Diprose	Saracens	England	2	0
K Bracken	Saracens	England	1	0
P Grayson	Northampton	England	1	0
T Stanger	Hawick	Scotland	1	0

You need a partner you can rely on.

Singer & Friedlander offers a wide range of
investment funds, PEPs and investment
management services.

To find out more simply telephone our
free investor helpline on 0500 505001. It
could be the start of a perfect partnership.

Singer & Friedlander
Investment Funds

Issued by Singer & Friedlander Investment Funds Ltd and Singer & Friedlander Portfolio Management Ltd, 21 New Street, London EC2M 4HR. Regulated by IMRO.

Reuters
DreamLions

MBN Promotions, sponsored by Reuters, created the concept of a Dream LIons team based on the best Lions Test players between 1971 and 1997. A panel of Willie John McBride, Ian Robertson, Phil Bennett, Gareth Chilcott and Cliff Morgan was invited to draw up a shortlist of the best sixty. They selected the following:

15.	J.P.R. Williams	Andy Irvine	Gavin Hastings	Neil Jenkins
14.	Gerald Davies	Andy Irvine	John Carleton	Ieuan Evans
13.	John Dawes	Mike Gibson	Ian McGeechan	Jeremy Guscott
12.	Ray Gravell	Clive Woodward	Dick Milliken	Scott Gibbs
11.	David Duckham	J.J. Williams	Roger Baird	Rory Underwood
10.	Barry John	Phil Bennett	John Rutherford	Rob Andrew
9.	Gareth Edwards	Robert Jones	Dewi Morris	Matt Dawson
1.	Iain McLauchlan	Fran Cotton	David Sole	Nick Popplewell
2.	Bobby Windsor	Peter Wheeler	Brian Moore	Keith Wood
3.	Sean Lynch	Graham Price	David Young	Jason Leonard
4.	Willie John McBride	Bill Beaumont	Paul Ackford	Martin Johnson
5.	Gordon Brown	Maurice Colclough	Wade Dooley	Jeremy Davidson
6.	Peter Dixon	Roger Uttley	Derek Quinnell	Mike Teague
7.	John Taylor	Fergus Slattery	Finlay Calder	Peter Winterbottom
8.	Mervyn Davies	Jeff Squire	Dean Richards	Tim Rodber

The final selection of the Reuters Dream Lions XV will be published on 19 December 1997 at the Reuters Dream Lions sporting luncheon at the Grosvenor House. However Ian McGeechan was invited to make his own personal selection for inclusion in this book.

It is always interesting to compare great players from different decades but it is also a rather dangerous exercise because so much has changed in the game between 1971 and 1997. In the end, I have made a purely subjective choice of the fifteen players from the eight British Lions tours since 1971 who I would most like to coach in a test against New Zealand, South Africa or Australia.

Just as we have done with the 1997 Lions, I have gone for specific combinations right through the team to give the best overall balance but always with the intention that we would be totally committed to playing fast open modern rugby under the current laws and in the style of the late 1990s. One thing never changes and the prerequisite for any team I would enjoy coaching is that the side is packed with talented footballers.

From the list of sixty players which has been presented to me there have been several positions where I have found it very difficult to make a decision but I have set up a list of priorities and in the final analysis I have selected for a match in 1997 rather than for 1971.

Even then I find it extremely hard to choose the perfect full back. The answer is really quite simple because in an ideal world I would want a mixture of the great strengths of JPR Williams, Andy Irvine and Gavin Hastings, but because no such hybrid actually exists, I have gone for JPR. He would not be as effective in attack or counter-attack as Andy or Gavin but taking every aspect of play into consideration he would have to rate the best. He had a tremendous physical presence and was rock solid in defence. He was also a strong-running full back who timed his entry into the line to perfection and there has never been a safer full back under the high ball.

On the right wing Gerald Davies had virtually everything. A master of deception, he had pace, acceleration, a shrewd brain and a devastating side-step. In defence, he might struggle against Jonah Lomu but most wings would. And, after all, we have got JPR at full back.

On the left wing there is precious little to choose between JJ Williams and David Duckham but I'll settle for JJ. He was not as a

Two complete footballers, JPR Williams with ball in hand and with Mike Gibson in support.

The incomparable Barry John and (right) Mervyn Davies watches as Gareth Edwards feeds the Lions.

even change the course of a game. He was super-confident and inspirational and he instilled confidence in everyone around him.

And that also applies to my choice at scrum half – Gareth Edwards. He had absolutely everything you could ever want in the complete scrum half. He is the automatic selection.

With such a multi-talented back division it is essential to have a strong, mobile pack. The forwards must be constructive and creative as well as technically sound. They need to be very good in the set-pieces and dynamic in the loose

natural a footballer but he was the ultimate try-taker. He was just about the best finisher in the game.

In the centre I have gone for the combination of Mike Gibson and Scott Gibbs. Mike was the most complete footballer of the last twenty-five years, equally outstanding in attack and defence, and a real thinker about the game. Alongside, for the best partnership, I go for the power, pace and strength of Scott Gibbs.

Fly half is even harder to choose than full back. I have long felt John Rutherford was the most underrated player of his time and I would place him right up there with the best. Rob Andrew helped the Lions win the Test series against Australia in 1989 and he also had a fine series against New Zealand in 1993. Phil Bennett was a brilliant match winner in 1974 and it was a privilege and a pleasure for me to play outside him on that tour in all four Tests. But, in the final analysis, I plump for Barry John. Barry was a genius. He could read a game better than anyone else and had an uncanny ability to take control of a game and

and in open play. My front-row choice would be Fran Cotton, Peter Wheeler and Graham Price.

Fran Cotton is one of only a handful of players in the last twenty-five years of international rugby who was just as formidable at loose-head or tight-head prop. To give the best balance and provide the best combination I have chosen him at loose head. In the modern game you still need size and power and you have to remember that for a big man he was also a very skillful player with good hands. With Fran we would have the best of both worlds – a big, strong scrummager who was good in the loose.

At hooker, I go for Peter Wheeler for the same reasons I went for Fran. In his day, he was big for a hooker but he was also a very clever player and the way the game is played now he would be in his element. He was a good footballer with excellent handling skills and he was a natural footballer. He was also a top class player when it came to throwing the ball into the line out.

At tight head I would complete the front row with another similar player in Graham Price. He was a magnificent scrummager who struck fear and trepidation into most loose-head props round the world and yet he had the speed and the footballing skills to score a try for Wales against France from one end of the pitch to the other. This front row gives us three good footballers but if any match developed into a physical battle it also gives us three of the toughest players I can think of.

The second row is not as straightforward a selection. It is very hard to leave out three locks who have all captained a British Lions tour to South Africa but if I am to stay consistent in my selection I have to go for Paul Ackford. There is no doubt Willie John McBride

Peter Wheeler, Fran Cotton and (inset) Graham Price, a formidable front row.

and Bill Beaumont were both great second-row forwards and great captains but they were the best in the game in the 1970s and the early 1980s and the game has moved on quite a lot since then.

For the modern game I believe Paul Ackford was the lock who changed the whole perception of the role of a front jumper. He had the ability as a big man to catch and control the ball at the front because he had the skill and timing to jump and win the ball cleanly. On the British Lions tour to Australia in 1989 we beat Queensland mainly because although we were being badly messed about in the middle and at the back, Paul won every single ball thrown to him at the front. He transformed the art of line out. He was also very mobile for such a big player and he read the game very well. He was one of those forwards who always seemed to be

Paul Ackford, who controlled the front of the line, and (right) Finlay Calder, an instinctive footballer.

in the right place at the right time.

Such a description also applies to Gordon Brown who is a player I would unhesitatingly choose as my middle jumper. He was a big man who had the size and the bulk to dominate the middle of the line out and the strength and the ballast to be a tremendous scrummager. But he was also a completely natural footballer. The son of a top-class goalkeeper, Gordon is a low-handicap golfer and apart from scoring eight tries on a Lions tour he was always in his element in the loose. In brief, he was the perfect all-round lock forward.

The choice at number eight is just as simple. Mervyn Davies had all the skills and natural ability to be the best player in that position in the '70s and he would also have been just as outstanding a player in the 1990s.

At blind-side flanker I would be very happy

with any of the four players on the short list because they each made an outstanding contribution to a Lions tour, but of the four the one I think would most relish the modern game is Peter Dixon. I have always felt he was a vastly underrated flanker and he was a player of immense talent. A big player, good at the back of the line out, he was also quick in the loose and had good hands.

Open-side flanker is equally difficult and again I would be very happy with any one of the four. In choosing Finlay Calder I am going for the most instinctive footballer of the four to make up the best combination in the back row alongside Peter Dixon and Mervyn Davies. Finlay had a nose for the ball and was always there. He knew exactly when to take the tackle

and when to pass, when to go into the ruck or maul and when to hang back. He was a great link player and always there in support. He was also, like all the other forwards I have chosen, a very tough cookie who always wanted to win.

I believe this team would be great fun to coach and would be capable of playing winning rugby at the very highest level.